Günter Hofbauer and Ruimei Zhou

Artificial Intelligence in Society

Also of interest

Artificial Intelligence in Higher Education.
Generative AI, Personalized Learning, Digital Transformation
Stamatios Papadakis, Georgios Lampropoulos (Eds.), 2026
ISBN 978-3-11-914829-0, e-ISBN (PDF) 978-3-11-220639-3,
e-ISBN (EPUB) 978-3-11-220640-9

Intelligent Educational Robots.
Toward Personalized Learning Environments
Stamatios Papadakis, Georgios Lampropoulos (Eds.), 2025
ISBN 978-3-11-135206-0, e-ISBN (PDF) 978-3-11-135269-5,
e-ISBN (EPUB) 978-3-11-135296-1

Industry 5.0.
A New Revolution Through Human-Centric Solution
Volume 17: De Gruyter Frontiers in Computational Intelligence
Yousaf Bin Zikria, Vinod Kumar Shukla, Pradeep N, Manoj Kumar M V, Harry Haoxiang Wang, Ali Kashif Bashir, 2025
ISBN 978-3-11-073955-8, e-ISBN (PDF) 978-3-11-073616-8,
e-ISBN (EPUB) 978-3-11-073623-6

Deep Learning for Cognitive Computing Systems.
Technological Advancements and Applications
Volume 7: Smart Computing Applications
M.G. Sumithra, Rajesh Kumar Dhanaraj, Celestine Iwendi and Anto Merline Manoharan (Eds.), 2023
ISBN 978-3-11-075050-8, e-ISBN (PDF) 978-3-11-075058-4,
e-ISBN (EPUB) 978-3-11-075061-4

Günter Hofbauer and Ruimei Zhou

Artificial Intelligence in Society

Automation, Human-Machine Interaction, Generative AI

DE GRUYTER

Authors
Prof. Dr Günter Hofbauer
Technical University Ingolstadt
Ingolstadt
Germany
Shenzhen Technology University
Shenzhen, Guangdong
China
E-mail: guenter.hofbauer@thi.de

Ruimei Zhou
Shenzhen Technology University
Shenzhen, Guangdong
China
E-mail: 2624786452@qq.com

ISBN 978-3-11-224271-1
ISBN 978-3-11-224272-8 (PDF)
ISBN 978-3-11-224273-5 (EPUB)
DOI https://doi.org/10.1515/9783112242728

Library of Congress Control Number: 2026938139

Bibliographic information published by the Deutsche Nationalbibliothek
The Deutsche Nationalbibliothek lists this publication in the Deutsche Nationalbibliografie;
detailed bibliographic data are available on the Internet at http://dnb.dnb.de.

De Gruyter and Walter de Gruyter GmbH are part of De Gruyter Brill.
www.degruyterbrill.com

Questions about General Product Safety Regulation:
productsafety@degruyterbrill.com

Cover illustration: agsandrew/iStock/Getty Images Plus

Preface

How Intelligent Machines Are Redefining Daily Living, Business, and What It Means to Be Human

Artificial intelligence (AI) is no longer a distant promise; it is the invisible architecture reshaping how we wake up, work, move, learn, and relate to one another. From the voice that adjusts our thermostat to the algorithms steering global supply chains, AI has injected unprecedented efficiency and convenience into everyday routines and entire industries. Yet its deepest impact lies beyond the merely technical: new business models are born, social norms are rewritten, and the rules of human-machine coexistence are being drafted in real time.

At home and in our pockets, AI delivers hyper-personalized medicine, on-demand education, and entertainment that learns our moods. Self-driving vehicles are not just safer cars; they are re-scripting the DNA of cities, turning traffic grids into fluid, data-driven ecosystems. But the deeper the integration, the starker the dilemmas: privacy evaporates, algorithms inherit our biases, and the digital divide widens into a chasm of new inequities. Each advance forces us to trust machines with decisions once reserved for humans, raising urgent questions about accountability, fairness, and the kind of society we want to code.

In the workplace, AI is simultaneously disruptor and catalyst. It vaporizes routine tasks while birthing roles that prize creativity, interdisciplinary insight, and ethical oversight. Fluency in data science and model optimization is becoming as fundamental as literacy once was. Leadership now means balancing ruthless efficiency with renewed empathy, guiding teams in which silicon and carbon colleagues learn from one another. Training and reskilling have broken free of rigid curricula; AI-driven, hyper-personal learning paths compress years of development into months. Yet algorithmic hiring and performance reviews risk freezing old prejudices into new code, and the privatization of core AI stacks threatens to concentrate power and opportunity in ever fewer hands.

This book is a field guide to that unfolding landscape. It maps how intelligent systems elevate the quality of life and turbo-charge productivity, while also confronting the ethical fault lines and social risks that accompany them. By dissecting current trends and hard choices, it invites readers to view AI not as a tool to be adopted but as a transformation to be shaped, one that demands collective stewardship by companies, policymakers, and citizens alike. Only through such shared vigilance can we ensure technology amplifies human values instead of eroding them, and can we craft a future where machines extend our capabilities without diminishing our humanity.

 | https://doi.org/10.1515/9783112242728-202

Contents

Chapter 1
Living with AI: The Quiet Takeover of Home, Habit, and Attention

Artificial intelligence (AI) is no longer knocking on the door of everyday life. It has already moved in, rearranged the furniture, and started learning our routines. From the moment we wake to the second we fall asleep, invisible algorithms modulate comfort, convenience, and even our sense of self.

The Smart Home That Knows You

Voice assistants, edge-computing hubs, and dense sensor networks now choreograph lighting, temperature, and security in real time. The result is an environment that adapts before we realize we are uncomfortable: blinds rise with circadian rhythms, air quality adjusts to pollen counts, and doors lock themselves when the last heartbeat leaves the room. Cleaning robots plot dust-maps; smart fridges track expiration dates and quietly reorder groceries. Wearable health monitors go further, turning living rooms into low-intensity clinics. By fusing heart-rate variability, sleep micro-movements, and ambient data, these devices detect incipient illness days before symptoms surface, shrinking the gap between early warning and medical intervention.

Yet seamlessness comes at a price. Fragmented IoT (Internet of Things) standards still make devices speak dialects, not just languages. More unsettling, the home becomes a data exhaust pipe: intimate patterns of respiration, conversation, and intimacy flow outward, demanding new architectures of privacy, on-device processing, federated learning, differential privacy, if domestic life is to remain private life.

Recommendation Engines That Shape Desire

Streaming services no longer wait for us to choose; they curate evenings, moods, even identities. Deep learning models compress decades of viewing behavior into micro-genres "rainy Tuesday Nordic noir with strong female lead" and auto-preview the next dopamine hit. E-commerce platforms perform the same sleight of hand on shopping carts, predicting needs before they surface in consciousness. Each click tightens the feedback loop between prediction and preference, raising engagement and the quiet risk of echo chambers that narrow your taste instead of expanding it.

Transparency and bias audits lag behind the speed of model iteration. When a recommendation goes wrong: say, a health supplement ad targeted to the newly bereaved, the harm feels personal, yet the mechanism remains opaque. The next fron-

 | https://doi.org/10.1515/9783112242728-001

tier is not just better algorithms, but accountable ones: dashboards that let users inspect, retrain, or mute the models that curate their lives.

From Tool to Companion

Natural language understanding, multimodal perception, and emotion recognition are dissolving the command-based interface. Assistants now infer intent beneath syntax: "It's cold" triggers not only a thermostat adjustment but also a suggestion to start the kettle and queue a playlist labeled "warmth." When sensors detect vocal stress, responses soften; when facial micro-expressions hint sadness, the assistant offers lighter music or a video call to a trusted friend.

The relationship is shifting from utility to companionship, raising urgent questions. If an AI can soothe loneliness, can it also deepen it by replacing human contact? Who owns the emotional profile built from thousands of late-night confessions? And what happens when the companion is accidentally or deliberately reprogrammed to serve someone else's agenda?

Time, Efficiency, and the Ethics of Convenience

AI compresses time: tasks that once filled weekends now vanish into background processes. Life becomes proactive rather than reactive; the thermostat learns, the inbox sorts itself, the car chooses the route before the driver thinks to ask. Yet efficiency without governance risks becoming its own tyranny. When systems optimize for speed or cost, they can erode autonomy, spontaneity, and serendipity, the very textures that make life feel human.

Convenience must be weighed against control, personalization against privacy, and human agency against machine autonomy. Designing the next decade of everyday AI is less a technical problem than a social contract: one that will be written in code, but must be ratified by citizens, regulators, and the technologists who currently hold the keys.

1.1 Intelligent Applications in Daily Life

AI technologies are increasingly stepping out of research labs and development centers to become an indispensable part of everyday life. From being woken up in the morning by voice assistants to having health devices monitor our sleep, AI shapes modern life in an invisible yet ever-present way. By simplifying tasks, predicting needs, and enhancing personalized services, these technologies transform complex challenges into almost effortless experiences.

Behind these cases lies not only a fireworks display of industrial innovation but also a rapid transformation of social structures. In this section, we will take a closer look at voice assistants, smart home systems, and health devices, analyze their value creation pathways, and discuss the central conflicts involved in the implementation of these technologies.

Intelligent Voice Assistants: Bridges Between Information and Action

Voice assistants have become a paragon of intelligent applications. Leveraging natural language processing (NLP) and speech synthesis technologies, they have elevated the experience of human-machine interaction to new heights. Voice assistants are not only tools for time management and information flow but also the core nexus connecting users to intelligent living solutions. Their intelligent networking and functional evolution are based on the following principles:

Context Awareness: Voice assistants do not merely interpret simple commands but provide context-specific recommendations through deep semantic and contextual understanding. For example, when providing flight details, they can automatically generate a travel checklist.

Proactive Adaptation: With the aid of machine learning, voice assistants can automatically tailor their services to user behavior, such as adjusting the timing of weather notifications or modifying language styles.

Cross-Device Responsiveness: They seamlessly synchronize requests across various devices, from smartphones to cars and smart home systems.

The proliferation of voice assistants reflects a positive alignment between technology and market demand but also reveals some challenges in implementation. The main challenges include:

Privacy and Trust: Continuous listening and necessary data storage raise significant privacy concerns. Even encrypted data can be compromised by service design or commercial motives.

Speech Recognition Inaccuracies: Insufficient support for different languages, accents, or users with disabilities can lead to social exclusion.

Striking a balance between intelligence and user trust is crucial for the widespread acceptance of voice assistants.

Smart Home: Deep Integration of Technology and Space

Smart homes are fundamentally transforming the concept of personal living spaces. Based on IoT technology, they connect various devices to create an automated and responsive living environment. They not only reduce the time demands of household management but also promote sustainable lifestyles.

As technological innovations and applications increase, the following issues are notable:

Demand Forecasting: With the help of deep learning algorithms, smart home devices can predict the needs of residents, such as adjusting room temperatures or pre-starting the coffee machine.
Energy Management: Through the collaboration of smart outlets, thermostats, and sensors, household energy consumption is optimized. Systems provide detailed reports and analyses that go beyond mere convenience to support sustainability goals.
From Siloed Solutions to Open Systems: Thanks to widely adopted open protocols, smart homes are breaking through brand barriers, allowing users to control devices from different manufacturers through a single platform.

However, the societal benefits and system-induced limitations need to be weighed, as despite their technological advantages, smart homes face challenges:
Uneven Distribution of Technology: Households with varying income levels show differing acceptance and usage rates, which can exacerbate the digital divide.
Compatibility and Update Issues: Despite the emphasis on openness, high update rates and inconsistent standards can increase long-term usage costs for users.
Environmental Concerns: Beyond the benefits of resource utilization, questions about the environmental impacts during production, use, and disposal phases are being raised.

The further development of smart homes should aim to promote social equity and resolve potential resource conflicts.

Health Devices: From Passive Monitoring to Active Intervention

Health monitoring devices are an ideal application area for AI. They enable the real-time visualization of health data and provide personalized improvement suggestions, which not only redefine health management but also give rise to new services in the medical field.

The prerequisites for technological realization and behavior shaping are as follows:
Data Fusion: Health devices integrate multimodal data sources such as body temperature, heart rate, and activity levels to create a comprehensive health profile. For example, smart wristbands combined with smartphone apps can create personalized training plans.
Proactive Mechanisms: Devices offer not only tracking but also functions based on behavioral model algorithms, such as health notifications that encourage users to develop positive habits.
Emergency Intervention: By quickly detecting anomalies, devices can send immediate alerts to medical facilities, thereby shortening intervention times and increasing rescue efficiency.

Despite the significant added value that health devices bring, the following difficulties need to be overcome:

Data Privacy and Security: As a central interface to the health system, sensitive data could cause considerable damage in the event of leaks or misuse. Stricter encryption standards and regulatory frameworks are required.

Intervention and Ethics: Automated health suggestions or mandatory monitoring could infringe on users' personal decision-making freedom, especially when third parties create specific intervention plans.

Monopolization of Health Resources: High technology and service costs could exclude certain population groups from benefiting from the innovation in the long term.

Health devices should not only be tools for improving individual life but also serve as bridges for more equitable and comprehensive health systems. For this, collaborative development of interconnected scenarios is necessary.

The extensive networking of smart devices not only shapes the user experience in individual scenarios but also creates the foundation for effective collaboration between different devices. Voice assistants can serve as the core control system for households, integrating both health monitoring and energy management into a unified control system. This synergistic effect offers added value that goes far beyond the functions of individual devices. The importance of technological integration can be illustrated by the following two points:

Interconnected Intelligent Networks: Supported by AI algorithms, devices can capture the finest details of the environment or user behavior and dynamically interact with each other, for example, by adjusting room lighting based on health data to improve sleep quality.

Expansion of Ecosystems: For example, by connecting to urban infrastructures, these devices can expand their application scope, such as in public transportation or community sharing services, to seamlessly connect households and urban systems.

The future vision here is: From Tool to Societal Enrichment. Because the increasing application of these technologies will not only improve individual life but also promote sustainable environmental and resource use through system efficiency. However, the responsibility to ensure transparency in algorithms and scientifically evaluate the societal impacts also increases.

Summary and Reflections

The deep integration of AI into everyday life demonstrates both the immense potential and the complex challenges of technological innovation. From user-friendliness to social responsibility, the dissemination of these technologies requires not only solutions to operational problems but also ethical guidance.

Striking a balance between innovation and regulation, comfort and data privacy, fairness and competition will be a long-term challenge. Achieving technological inclusion and creating a caring ecosystem are decisive steps toward a smarter and more equitable future.

1.2 Personalized Recommendations and Data-Driven Decisions

With the increasing maturity of data-driven technologies, personalized recommendation systems have become an essential bridge between user needs and data-driven experiences: The core logic of recommendation systems!

Whether in the realm of shopping, entertainment, or education recommendation systems analyze in-depth data to create personalized experiences for users. This not only enhances their satisfaction but also changes the rules of entire industries.

The core logic of recommendation systems can be divided into three main modules: data collection, behavioral analysis, and recommendation generation. First, the system comprehensively collects data on user behavior, social interactions, geographical locations, and even device settings. Subsequently, it builds predictive models using collaborative filtering algorithms, content-based algorithms, or hybrid models. Finally, the system delivers products, services, or content that match the needs and preferences of users.

Algorithms and Business Models in Combination

The outstanding performance of recommendation systems is based on the close integration of algorithms and business models. For example, Netflix uses predictive models based on its users' viewing habits to recommend customized content, thereby optimizing both user satisfaction and business results. Similarly, Amazon employs personalized recommendations, which account for about 35% of its sales. The success lies not only in the nature of the recommendations but also in the precise analysis of data ecosystems and user behavior.

Despite the clear advantages, recommendation systems face challenges such as the invisibility of their algorithms. The prediction processes within these systems are often black-box models, making it impossible for users to perceive the weightings and impacts of the recommendations. Moreover, the widespread data collection leads to an increased dependence on user privacy, which intensifies the call for greater transparency.

Application Areas: Changing the Rules of Shopping, Entertainment, and Learning

Precise Recommendations in the Shopping Domain

Personalized recommendation technologies are deeply integrated into e-commerce platforms and significantly enhance the efficiency and satisfaction of purchase decisions through user profiling, behavioral analysis, and preference prediction. For example, when a user is searching for fitness equipment, the system might recommend matching sportswear, nutritional supplements, or a discount package of complementary products. This predictive capability can uncover hidden user needs and drive purchasing decisions that users might not have initially considered.

In addition to increasing the likelihood of purchases, the system creates added value for products that are not directly searched for through the "long-tail effect." Niche items, such as obscure books or limited-edition electronics, gain importance through enhanced visibility, allowing merchants to better balance sales targets and customer satisfaction.

However, the challenge of the "echo chamber effect" remains. If preferences and user behavior are strongly confined to closed loops, the system may excessively reinforce dominant interests and neglect the diversity of user experiences. Algorithm developers face the task of finding the right balance between personalization and diversity.

Prioritization in the Entertainment Sector

The entertainment industry has undergone significant changes through personalized recommendations. Platforms such as Netflix, Spotify, and YouTube use predictive algorithms to optimize the user experience in content consumption and reduce the burden of decision-making. For example, Spotify offers a "Daily Mix" that combines musical preferences with emotional scenarios to provide tailored content.

In addition to increasing user engagement, recommendation systems have also shaped new business models. Netflix designs its homepage with short video previews and recommendation logic to increase the time users spend on the platform. At the same time, content providers can base their production decisions on predictions of user interactions, such as likes and playback frequency.

However, ethical issues can also be exacerbated. One example is algorithmic bias, which could lead to a monotonous selection of content, such as the continuous promotion of extreme content. In highly commercialized scenarios, recommendations might focus more on content with high advertising revenue rather than on the actual needs or maximum benefit of users, a tension that can affect the quality of information.

Optimizing Learning Pathways in the Education Sector

Amidst the continuous evolution of educational innovation, personalized recommendations are progressively emerging as a driving force for efficient learning processes.

Platforms such as Coursera and Khan Academy monitor learning progress, problem-solving rates, and other parameters in real time to create flexible learning pathways that facilitate structured knowledge transfer.

Compared to traditional curriculum plans, learning pathways optimized through recommendation systems exhibit greater adaptability. For instance, novice programmers can receive modules recommended at a difficulty level, which commensurates with their knowledge base, thereby reducing potential gaps in knowledge transfer and enhancing overall efficiency.

However, the short-term orientation of algorithms may curb learners' potential. Prioritizing the delivery of easily understandable content could marginalize challenging modules, thereby missing the long-term educational goal of overcoming cognitive barriers. These contradictions demand that education practitioners proactively integrate incentives and diversity into their algorithms.

Relevant Data Privacy and Ethical Issues

Recommendation systems are highly dependent on user data, which inevitably gives rise to data privacy issues. The challenge lies in balancing privacy and transparency, as data collection often occurs without the knowledge of users. For instance, e-commerce platforms may not only analyze users' search behavior but also combine data from voice assistants and social media, a lack of transparency that makes it difficult to delineate the boundaries of data usage.

Moreover, the algorithms of recommendation systems are often closed in their mode of operation, making it impossible for users to assess commercially motivated interests within the systems. For example, sales platforms may prioritize recommendations for products with high advertising placements, which may not align with user needs. This deficit in transparency is a serious weakness in the trust of the technology.

Algorithmic Bias and Fairness

A challenging ethical aspect of recommendation systems is their potential bias due to poor data or inadequate model design. For example, recruitment platforms might use historical behavioral data that leads to the disadvantage of certain groups, such as gender or ethnic minorities. Educational platforms might favor content for major languages, thereby excluding smaller target groups.

The key to reducing algorithmic bias is the transparent restructuring of data and models. Training datasets should be as diverse as possible, and the model should actively implement fairness constraints to promote a discrimination-free prediction method. These adjustments not only fix technical errors but also support societal fairness.

Perspectives

In the long term, the establishment of transparency and fairness should be pursued as a goal. The future of personalized recommendation technologies is both responsible and promising. The following approaches can help to achieve a balance between technology, user experience, and ethics:

Explainable Models (explainable AI) for Transparency: Develop interpretable AI models that are understandable for both users and regulatory authorities, enabling code-level scrutiny.

Integration of Fairness Indicators and Modifications: Promote fairness research in algorithms to eliminate social biases and balance business and social objectives.

Recommendation of Privacy-Preserving Technologies: Utilize technologies such as differential privacy or federated learning to protect sensitive data while maintaining privacy.

Enrichment of Diversity and Introduction of Random Mechanisms: Incorporate diversity factors into recommendations to expand user experiences and minimize the "monotony of suggestions."

Conclusion

Personalized recommendation systems not only reflect the immense potential of AI but also point to possible risks and ethical challenges. The interaction between technology, ethics, and legislation will be crucial in determining whether these systems promote social progress or exacerbate existing problems in the data-driven era. The search for the intersection of technology and responsibility remains the central task for future digital innovators.

1.3 The Evolution of Human-Machine Interaction Design

Human-machine interaction is undergoing a profound transformation, evolving from simple, command-based exchanges to richer, understanding-driven dialogues. Propelled by the rapid advance of AI, the objective is no longer merely to satisfy functional requirements, but to genuinely comprehend human language, emotion, and behavior.

From Command-Based to Understanding-Based Interaction

This section highlights breakthroughs in NLP and emotion recognition, their practical deployment, and the pivotal challenges that accompany real-world adaptation: privacy, algorithmic fairness, and seamless integration into everyday and professional life.

Natural Language Processing: A Bridge Between Technology and Human Language

NLP architectures serve as a technological bridge, endowing machines with the ability to understand, generate, and process human language. Below, we examine their concrete applications and design challenges in human-machine interaction:

Chatbots and Intelligent Assistants as Core Tools of the Connected Experience

Contemporary chatbots and intelligent assistants, ChatGPT, Alexa, Google Assistant, are pushing interaction from single-purpose functionality to multitasking and cognitive engagement. Progress is measured not only by accurate responses, but by real-time context handling and task optimization. A hotel-booking program equipped with a language-aware assistant, for instance, can infer nuanced preferences from past user behavior and recommend premium rooms plus tailored services.

Yet the underlying technical hurdles are formidable. While conversational systems increasingly strive for logical coherence, their grasp of cultural and linguistic nuance remains limited. In multilingual settings, slang or emotionally charged speech can create stark disparities in user experience. Transparent algorithms and refined semantic-analysis models are required to close these gaps incrementally.

Real-Time Translation: Emotional Connection Through Globalized Technology

Real-time translation tools, such as the enhanced version of Google Translate, now do more than just enable global communication; they are gaining contextual sensitivity. In business conversations, they can capture tone and speaking style, minimizing communication barriers arising from linguistic differences.

Progress, however, raises questions of data dependence. Global systems demand vast quantities of real-world data, sparking concerns about privacy and cultural respect. In linguistically diverse regions like Africa and Asia, machine translations often overlook local, ethical and cultural nuances, making this a critical frontier for algorithm design.

Context-Aware Systems: Deep Capture of Language and User States

Advanced NLP technologies are integrating contextual cues into interaction. Smart home appliances can fuse historical usage patterns with current environmental data to decode “the intent behind the words,” proactively anticipating and understanding user needs rather than merely executing commands.

These systems carry inherent risks. Misclassification of context or intent can yield inaccurate recommendations and degraded experiences. Multi-stage validation mechanisms within semantic models are therefore essential to secure and strengthen decision logic.

Emotional Computing: A Perceptual Revolution Beyond Interaction

As a cornerstone of understanding-based interaction, emotional computing extends machine perception beyond language, enabling recognition of the emotions embedded in speech, gestures, and behavior. The result is interaction design with heightened humanity.

The Industrialization of Emotional Intelligence

Emotion recognition technologies are now deployed across mental health services and customer experience optimization. In healthcare, AI assistants can assess a patient's psychological state, such as anxiety or depression levels, by analyzing voice and facial cues, then tailor communication styles accordingly. This addresses the traditional shortcoming of overlooking emotional data, making doctor-patient interaction more efficient and precise.

A central challenge remains distinguishing complex emotional states. An utterance may simultaneously exhibit features of anxiety and excitement, which traditional systems struggle to parse, leading to error-prone evaluations. Emotional algorithms must therefore evolve from one-dimensional detection to cross-modal understanding models.

Accessible Interaction: Best Practices

In retail, emotion recognition is embedded in intelligent customer service applications that detect vocal nervousness or anger and adapt interaction strategies on the fly. This improves real-time problem resolution and strengthens user trust. Conversely, misinterpreted emotions can breach trust if algorithmic logic diverges from genuine user needs.

Converging Creative Domains for Emotional Stimulation

Emotion recognition also opens new avenues in art and design. In generative AI, dynamic models driven by user emotion can predict needs and create artifacts, advertising copy, product packaging that users may not have consciously sought. This redefines design processes and fosters more diverse forms of human–machine collaboration.

Technological Realization and Real-World Challenges

Implementing understanding-based interactions is not a purely technical endeavor; it demands resolving contradictions at the technological, ethical, and societal levels.

Precision vs. Risk of Misinterpretation

Even the most advanced natural language and emotion-computing systems cannot completely rule out misreading user intent. A financial-services chatbot, for example, might mistakenly interpret financial stress as high purchasing power, eroding customer trust. A dynamic framework that continuously refines its recognition logic through user feedback is therefore essential.

Privacy and the Trust Crisis

Understanding-driven interactions require vast datasets, behavioral patterns, voice recordings, and more, which might raise privacy risks. Misuse or leakage of user data could severely impede the adoption of intelligent technologies. Differential privacy or federated learning can enable tailored interaction design that safeguards sensitive data while still delivering user-centric services.

Technological Dependence and Loss of Personal Agency

As intelligent interaction design grows more sophisticated, there is a risk that active exploration by users devolves into passive consumption. Household appliances that predict needs with uncanny accuracy may reduce users' motivation to understand the underlying technology. This "technological laziness" could foster unhealthy dependence and shape long-term behavioral development. Designers must balance smart assistance with user autonomy, ensuring that design logic never drifts too far from human needs.

Future Outlook: From Tools to Collaborative Partners

The evolution of understanding-based interactions is transforming not only the form of technology but also the relationship between humans and machines.

Expanding Application Domains through Multimodal Interaction

Tomorrow's interaction technologies will fuse visual, verbal, and contextual information to deliver seamless multimodal experiences. Already under development are in-vehicle systems that combine driver emotion, external conditions (road surface, weather), and driving habits to adjust warnings and driving modes in real time.

Cultural Diversity and Fair Interaction

Global deployment of understanding-based systems demands heightened cultural sensitivity. The open question is how algorithms can correctly interpret communication styles across cultures while avoiding cultural bias. Algorithm development and dataset curation must therefore prioritize diversity and fairness.

Explainability and an Ethical Framework

As these technologies exert greater influence, interpretable models that let users understand system decisions become critical. Ethical-governance mechanisms, certifying that algorithms uphold fairness principles and integrating transparency into decision processes, will play a pivotal role.

Conclusion: Interaction Design for an Intelligent Connection

Human-machine interaction design is evolving into a bridge between technological progress and societal change. It is no longer merely command-driven; it is paving the way for a complex, collaborative future between humans and technology. Advances in understanding-based interaction narrow the gap between technology and humanity, providing sustainable momentum for commercial innovation, public services, and personal experiences. Yet privacy protection and ethical fairness must remain integral to ensure that the human-technology relationship is empowering rather than constraining. On the road to a visualized future, designers and users together will define the boundaries of an intelligent society.

1.4 Automation and Job Enrichment

AI, armed with powerful data processing and algorithmic capabilities, is fundamentally reshaping the entire work ecosystem. Its dual impact on boosting efficiency and unleashing creativity has already transformed both daily life and professional environments.

Through the widespread adoption of intelligent automation technologies, especially RPA (robotic process automation), repetitive tasks can now be completed at unprecedented speed and precision. Examples range from high-volume financial-transaction processing to data analysis and forecasting in logistics management. This not only lowers operating costs but also forces organizations to question and redesign traditional processes and work patterns in pursuit of simultaneous gains in efficiency and effectiveness.

At the same time, new tools such as generative AI significantly enhance workplace innovation by optimizing creative workflows and reducing the cost of turning ideas into reality. Technologies that automatically generate design templates or surface potential inspirations from massive datasets free individuals to devote more time and mental space to critical thinking.

Yet these efficiency and creativity gains do not come without challenges. Large-scale deployment of technology delivers scalable ways of working, yet it can also rigidify innovation paths. On the one hand, excessive reliance on existing algorithmic optimizations may limit cognitive diversity and dampen the willingness to explore unconventional approaches. On the other hand, collaborating with technology requires people to upgrade their skills continuously, which can create an over-dependence on tools and blur the independence of creative workers. Most crucially, workplace creativity must strike a dynamic balance between "technological assistance" and "independent freedom"; otherwise, technology risks shifting from supporter to dominant voice.

From a management perspective, an AI-driven change compels organizations to rethink resource-allocation principles and employee role structures. The redistribution of work content no longer follows traditional competency hierarchies; instead, it focuses on leveraging the respective comparative advantages of human and machine intelligence. Leaders must encourage employees to concentrate on high-value areas that are difficult to quantify such as strategic planning and deep innovation. Meanwhile, AI-driven data transparency and decentralization are replacing hierarchical management with flatter, more agile organizational structures.

Whether technological advances can be smoothly integrated into the workplace and whether effective human-machine collaboration can emerge ultimately depends on cultural orientation and ethical leadership. If efficiency is pursued one-sidedly while value orientations are neglected, human potential will be wasted and instrumentalization tendencies will intensify, leading to the side effect of "technological coldness." Therefore, performance evaluation must move beyond a purely technical dimension and embed humanistic concerns into managerial decisions, ensuring that technology is not merely an efficiency tool but a key force for promoting social inspiration and justice. Only by integrating ethics and culture can AI be transformed into true "intelligent momentum" for social progress and create a more harmonious future in everyday life.

Drivers of Change

Automation technologies are powerful engines of change in the world of work. Their rapid development not only allows companies to use resources more efficiently and boost productivity, but also quietly redefines the very meaning of "work." From early mechanical operation to today's AI-based intelligent decision support, automation drives organizations to look beyond cost and efficiency toward higher-order goals of value creation and ecological sustainability.

The hallmark of modern automation lies in its intelligence and flexibility. It is not merely a substitute for repetitive labor; it also performs complex tasks optimally and acts as an innovation partner. In industrial contexts, automation technologies help firms to solve highly complex problems quickly and precisely, challenges that traditional methods struggle to address, while simultaneously freeing employees to focus on strategic and creative activities.

Microsoft's Copilot tool, for example, leverages generative AI to give knowledge workers intelligent support in creating and analyzing content, significantly reducing the time spent on routine documentation and report generation.

Tesla's automated production lines demonstrate how precise algorithms and robotic technology can achieve efficient delivery and cost optimization.

These technological innovations deliver economic benefits and also stimulate profound reflection on the future of work.

Companies that deploy automation technologies, however, need both long-term strategic planning and a clear understanding of technological limits. AI can certainly analyze vast datasets in depth, yet its insights remain bounded by the scope and quality of the data. Moreover, the successful implementation of automation solutions rarely proceeds smoothly; its success depends critically on the openness of corporate culture and employees' acceptance of new technologies.

From Repetitive Labor to Intelligent Augmentation: The Turning Point in the World of Work

Traditional automation focused almost exclusively on replacing repetitive, labor-intensive, low-value tasks, e.g., assembly-line work in manufacturing or parcel-sorting in logistics. This "mechanistic substitution" delivered clear efficiency gains for highly standardized, recurrent operations. Yet, by its very nature, it was narrow in scope and quickly reached its limits.

With the infusion of AI, modern automation has ascended to an entirely new level: one of intelligent augmentation. It now tackles assignments that demand dynamic adaptation and the orchestration of complex processes. In production monitoring, for example, computer vision technology has expanded quality inspection from merely flagging defective items to predictive maintenance: by mining large historical datasets, it spots potential faults long before they occur. Likewise, deep learning algorithms in medical diagnostics can scan tens of thousands of images and highlight anomalies with a speed and precision that surpass human experts.

The significance of this inflection point is that automation no longer just substitutes mechanically repeatable work; it increasingly assumes the entire "analysis-decision-execution" chain. Organizations must, however, remain alert to two central risks. First, technology uncertainty, especially in high-stakes domains such as medicine or aviation, where even tiny deviations can have catastrophic consequences. Second, the widening gap between rapid technological progress and the comparatively slow adaptation of human skills and organizational structures, which can erode overall efficiency.

From Data Management to Insight Generation

Within the automation revolution, Intelligent Decision Support Systems (IDSS) serve as a crucial intermediary layer, enabling companies to extract actionable insights from oceans of data. IDSS combine machine learning algorithms, NLP, and visualization technologies to reveal deeply hidden patterns and to offer strategic recommendations and concrete action proposals.

A prominent case is Amazon's warehouse management system, which integrates global supply chain data with consumer behavior patterns to forecast market demand in real time and to optimize inventory dynamically. The result is less waste and a more responsive supply chain. The banking sector also benefits: IDSS tools not only flag fraud and risk early, but also help optimize complex investment portfolios.

The strength of IDSS lies in delivering "insights," not ready-made "decisions." They illuminate possibilities, yet the final call still demands human judgment in specific contexts. For successful implementation, firms must therefore address three key issues: high-quality data (crucial for algorithmic effectiveness), model transparency (to keep algorithmic choices explainable and trustworthy), and robust privacy policies (to meet public concerns about ethical technology use).

Returning Automation to Its True Purpose

In strategic planning and deployment, a common fear is that automation will damage labor markets. A closer look reveals that automation's real value lies in complementing human labor, not in replacing it outright. It boosts efficiency, yet should never diminish the unique worth of human work.

A classic example is medical diagnostics. AI systems can analyze vast quantities of imaging data in minutes, yet tasks such as the psychological care of patients, the integration of personal medical histories, and the crafting of individualized treatment plans remain the province of physicians. This "human-machine complementarity model" accelerates diagnostic workflows while allowing medical staff to devote more attention to humane care and innovative developments.

The core question is how to redefine the purpose of automation: not as a "competing rival," but as a "co-operative partner." Complex human capabilities like emotion, creativity, and moral judgment remain indispensable in the workplace. Automation should amplify human potential rather than supplant it.

The New Automation Vision: Opportunities and Challenges

Future applications of automation will span numerous sectors: precision-controlled, unmanned agricultural machinery; dynamic traffic management in smart cities; generative AI for industrial design; and personalized customer service interactions. Enabled by profound technological empowerment, we can optimize resource utilization and maximize societal benefit across diverse scenarios.

Yet the challenges are equally impressive. In a sensitive labor market, certain activities will inevitably be displaced by automation, while the pace of upskilling and reskilling struggles to keep up with rapid technological change. Data privacy, technological transparency, and workers' rights sit at the center of industry regulation. If neglected, long-term automation gains could be curtailed by social backlash and even societal upheaval.

Conclusion: Steering Technological Progress with Wisdom and Responsibility

Automation technology is a double-edged sword: it can revolutionize productivity, yet also challenge social stability. When introducing automated systems, companies must place people at the center, creating an ecosystem that is beneficial for all stakeholders. Policymakers and industry leaders alike must shoulder responsibility, guiding technology toward fairness and sustainability.

The ultimate yardstick for automation is not the steepness of the efficiency curve or the level of the return on investment, but the extent to which it makes society wiser and more inclusive. Looking ahead, we must hold fast to the conviction that technology is a means to craft better worlds of work. In this era of harmony between technology and the workplace, human judgment and accountability will write the final chapter of the story.

1.5 The Imperative to Redefine Job Profiles

The rise of AI is reshaping daily life and the professional ecosystem, undermining the foundations of traditional roles while unlocking growth potential for innovative approaches. These changes are not confined to the technical layer; they are also recasting the architecture of corporate culture and professional ethics. By deeply analyzing role shifts, the emergence of new positions, and the turbulence of transition, we can examine how to seize the opportunities of a technology-driven realignment of careers, while simultaneously building a more resilient future for individuals and organizations.

Deep-Seated Transformations of the World of Work Triggered by AI

The AI-induced upheaval in the workplace can be viewed as a key milestone in the transition from the industrial to the intelligent era. Repetitive, rule-bound tasks are increasingly ceded to machines, freeing space for innovation and decision-making. Automated systems, intelligent algorithms, and generative tools not only raise the efficiency of enterprise operations but also profoundly influence how people work and what they understand “a job” to mean.

Traditional employment fields are reaching for technical competency extensions, while harder-to-measure capabilities, data-driven insight, and creative problem-solving are becoming the core values of new positions. As enterprises strive to explore new paths in the dynamic equilibrium between human and machine, the AI-propelled professional ecosystem grows more flexible, more complex, and richer in opportunity.

Job Displacement and Transformation: Structural Change

Over the past decades, positions that demanded substantial human and temporal resources have been evaluated, and largely replaced, by a fresh wave of automation. AI technologies, through high-frequency, precise, and low-cost simulations, have placed production lines, information processing, and back-office support at the top of the change list.

In finance, traditional auditors are being superseded by automated audit tools. These solutions use NLP and semantic analysis to spot anomalies and risk points in vast transaction data at speeds and accuracies far beyond human reach.

In transport and logistics, drones and warehouse robots are progressively taking over roles whose tasks were once fixed and manual.

Yet, as these activities disappear, the resources they release inject new momentum into industries, spurring roles of higher added value and lower repetitiveness. The transformation is both challenge and chance.

Upward Trajectories for Traditional Professions

Although automation eliminates many purely operational roles, it simultaneously drives the further evolution of traditional professions.

Mechanical engineers must now master not only device hardware but also the associated control software and integration with IoT devices.

Accountants are morphing into financial system management experts who, armed with AI-based analytic tools, move far beyond report generation to provide strategic decision support.

Behind these competency upgrades lies a clear trend: positions are not simply erased; rather, they are upgraded from low-value stages to technology-driven strategic partners. Employees must dynamically recalibrate career goals and adapt to the new fusion of technology and work.

1.6 New Professions and Multidisciplinary Role Requirements

Data-driven mindsets and algorithm-centric design are accelerating the expansion of entirely new technical career paths. Data, often labeled the new oil or the electricity of the twenty-first century, have become the decisive engine behind the redefinition of professional roles. Positions such as data scientists, machine learning engineers, and model optimization specialists now represent the fastest-growing job families. One example is the data science team at a major retail group that balances complex demand signals with required inventory levels by means of deep learning models.

Beyond that, AI model trainers take responsibility for the iterative development of models on the basis of large datasets while simultaneously auditing their compliance and fairness and even drafting ethical guidelines for the models themselves. Data-driven roles are therefore driving comprehensive change in both depth and breadth.

Multidisciplinary Roles: Resonance Between Technology and the Humanities

AI is no longer the exclusive domain of engineers; its far-reaching application requires the collaboration of multidisciplinary roles. As generative AI enters sensitive areas, many companies now appoint AI-ethics officers to ensure that technologies conform to social norms and legal requirements. These officers need not only technical knowledge but also solid grounding in management and the social sciences to coordinate technology teams with diverse stakeholder groups.

Another promising multidisciplinary role is that of the "Manager for Technology and Business Communication." This position functions as a liaison between technical teams and organizational strategy, translating complex technical concepts into commercially viable applications while converting business objectives into technical plans. The emergence of such roles underscores the importance of a coexistence model between technology and the humanities within the value chain.

Conflicts of Transformation: Challenges and Mechanisms

An imbalance between competency requirements and psychological tensions calls for a solution. The rapid redefinition of professional roles has exposed a rift between technological progress and workforce adaptability. Many employees feel insecure, even resistant about the transition; they lack basic AI literacy and may lose confidence in their future careers. One survey shows that more than 70% of traditional employees believe AI poses a threat to their future work, yet fewer than 30% are actively acquiring new skills.

Technological change can also trigger cultural conflicts within organizations, from executives accustomed to traditional management methods to front-line employees confronted by skill deficits. AI's rapid penetration requires a more inclusive organizational culture model to enable successful role transformation.

Creating a Future-Oriented Learning Ecosystem

The core of conflict resolution lies in establishing mechanisms for continuous learning and competency development. Multidimensional learning approaches already demonstrate strong potential in practice. AI-driven personalized training systems can design tailored learning paths for different industries and positions. Short-term boot camps, online courses, and intensive workshops are likewise critical components for closing technical skill gaps.

Enterprises and governments must work together to develop socially supportive measures not only by strengthening educational systems to cultivate technical talent, but also by implementing reskilling programs and professional transition initiatives for sectors heavily affected by job displacement.

Insight: Dynamic Equilibrium Between Technological Transformation and Human Care

The process of AI-driven career redefinition is undoubtedly a systemic challenge and transformation. Yet the heart of the world of work will remain human. Technology is merely a tool; the real question is how to deploy it wisely to strengthen ourselves and to create added value for organizations. That is the ultimate goal of transformation.

Conclusion

In the future, companies must act as mediators between technology deployment, employee adaptability, and organizational ethics; individuals must actively embrace new technologies and acquire new skills through learning; policymakers must ensure that the benefits of technology are distributed fairly. Through collaboration we can not only accept new definitions of professions but also foster a world of work that is smarter, fairer, and more humane.

Technology can change work, but what truly defines work is humanity's claim to meaning and value. That may be the central question worth pondering in the age of AI.

1.7 How Creativity Benefits from Intelligent Tools

Creativity is the driving force behind societal progress and technological innovation. Against the backdrop of rapid advances in AI, intelligent tools have not only dramatically improved the efficiency with which repetitive work is off-loaded; they have also fundamentally expanded the depth and breadth of creative practice. From generative AI models to automated research platforms, technological progress compels society as a whole: individuals, companies, and institutions alike to rethink how value is created and to redraw the boundaries of innovation. This section examines the multidimensional ways in which AI supports creativity, analyzes the key dilemmas that accompany the deployment of these technologies, and outlines the challenges that must be addressed.

Freeing Creativity from Repetitive Tasks

Creative processes are often constrained by a host of repetitive activities. While these steps may be necessary, they divert the creator's time and energy away from the truly innovative core. As a tool, AI not only handles these foundational tasks but also enables a sharper focus on the pivotal phases of innovation.

In the visual arts domain, AI capabilities in creative software have already produced remarkable results. Generative in-painting, for instance, analyzes the surrounding context and extrapolates to fill in missing parts of an image automatically. Professional designers can therefore concentrate on overarching stylistic direction and thematic development rather than on painstaking detail work. The technology also lowers entry barriers, allowing less-experienced users to participate in high-level creative projects. Similar tools are now applied in video editing and advertising production, dissolving the traditional limitation of creativity to a small circle of experts.

In engineering, generative design technologies, such as those embedded in Autodesk's "Generative Design," extend the possibilities of industrial design. Algorithms automatically generate numerous solution alternatives and identify the optimal configuration in real time. Engineers are thus less constrained by conventional standard models and can more freely explore novel design possibilities. This automation not only boosts efficiency but also multiplies the diversity and creative freedom available in the design process.

Generative AI and the Spark for New Creative Frontiers

Generative AI has established itself as the central engine for elevating creative output. By means of deep learning methods, it can simulate and understand human creative patterns at scale, enabling end-to-end support from ideation to the complete re-creation of content. Text generation tools such as OpenAI's GPT-5 can produce coherent and richly detailed copy in seconds, while image generation tools like DALL-E translate user prompts into complex visual effects, vastly expanding the possibilities of digital creativity. Advertising agencies, for instance, use these tools to create a wide range of visual assets and textual drafts, accelerating the creative process and seeding new directions of thought.

Yet, despite its broad applicability, generative AI's breakthrough creativity still relies on the deeper emotional expressiveness and abstract human interpretations that machines cannot yet replicate. This exposes a central paradox: while AI is extraordinarily productive at generating novel patterns, it struggles to produce truly groundbreaking artworks. Amper Music is a case in point, the platform can generate technically flawless background music, but it lacks a musician's cultural perspective and emotional depth, thereby limiting the uniqueness of the art. This tension underscores the necessity of combining intelligent tools with the sensory experience of human creators in order to unlock a fuller creative potential.

Deeper Integration of Technology and Creative Practice: Collaboration Drives Innovation

AI-powered creative tools are not merely technical aids; they reinforce a new "human-machine collaboration" working model. Intelligent layout and generative technologies embedded in design software give creative teams more efficient pathways for idea generation instead of presenting only individual solutions. UI/UX design tools, for example, support teams by real-time optimization of design proposals, allowing high-quality prototypes to be developed quickly and then further refined. These collaborative approaches increase the consistency of creative processes within teams while also freeing space for strategic planning and future-oriented exploration.

Similar innovation patterns are spreading to interdisciplinary cooperation. The online collaboration platform Miro, for instance, combines NLP with knowledge management technologies to organize brainstorming outputs and identify efficient solutions. Such tools not only boost team productivity but also create scientifically grounded decision foundations through deep data analysis. The challenge, however, lies in cultivating a workplace culture that embraces these new collaborative approaches and in ensuring that team members are adaptable to modern working methods.

Automated Research Platforms Propel Innovation

Creativity is not confined to the arts; it is equally vital in scientific research and technological development. AI-powered, fully automated research platforms have already transformed traditional innovation pipelines.

In drug discovery, for example, deep learning models can rapidly screen millions of molecular structures and predict promising active compounds in weeks rather than months. AlphaFold's breakthrough in protein structure prediction has likewise revolutionized molecular biology.

In the social sciences, dynamic scenario analysis tools now simulate complex social variables in real time, helping policy makers to craft forward-looking strategies. Yet these creative accelerators also introduce challenges, ethical risks, and algorithmic bias. Skewed data can yield flawed models, and over-reliance on automation may erode scientists' capacity for independent, deep-dive analysis.

Beyond the Tool: How Intelligent Technologies Elevate Creativity

The value of intelligent tools lies not only in task execution but in expanding creative frontiers and overturning entrenched mindsets. Virtual reality and advanced visualization platforms let creators render abstractions that were once impossible to depict, replacing the old paradigm: "creation ends when the artifact is finished," with dynamic adaptation and real-time feedback.

Smart urban planning software, fed with granular climate data, enables engineers to forecast environmental changes and optimize sustainable designs. In the creative economy, artists fuse intelligent tools with interdisciplinary concepts to produce works that are more influential and multi-layered. These practices demonstrate a symbiotic relationship between technology and project vision, transcending purely utilitarian tool thinking.

Challenges in Democratizing Creativity

As intelligent tools proliferate, creativity is being made accessible on a scale never seen before. AI-powered educational platforms and creative applications now allow people without specialized backgrounds to take part in creative processes. Personalized learning paths can be tailored to different skill levels, enabling users to master complex capabilities, such as image generation or text creation within days. This marks a transition from professionalized work to everyday, popular creativity.

Yet the democratization of creativity also introduces challenges in quality control and technological ethics. Intelligent tools can mechanize creative workflows, leading to stylistic homogenization. Over-simplified creation methods may tempt users to abandon deep refinement of ideas. To meet these challenges, developers must balance openness with guardrails, and users must safeguard their creative standards through continuous professional development.

Conclusion: Intelligent Tools as Catalysts for Creativity

The goal of AI is not to dictate the boundaries of creativity, but to act as a catalyst that expands human thinking. As intelligent technologies become ever more embedded in our creative processes, the critical question is not only which problems they solve, but how they reshape our understanding of what a problem is. In the future, the ideal relationship between AI and human creativity should be symbiotic rather than adversarial.

Therefore, when implementing these technologies, we must ensure they do not foster excessive dependence that narrows our cognitive horizons. The true value of creativity lies in breaking conventional boundaries; the mission of intelligent tools is to facilitate this breakthrough and to connect technology with human emotion. The challenge for today's creative ecosystem is to reconcile tool efficiency with intellectual depth in a technology-driven age, thereby opening new avenues for innovation and change.

1.8 From Routine Tasks to Peak Capabilities

AI is accelerating the global redefinition of work, offering unprecedented opportunities while simultaneously posing profound challenges. As automated technologies penetrate every sector, repetitive, process-based tasks are increasingly displaced, and demand for talent is shifting toward higher-value cognitive skills and multidimensional competencies. The key competence of tomorrow's jobs is the ability to reskill, how individuals move from easily replaceable, technical tasks to more creative, strategic, and collaborative roles.

Consequently, dynamic societies now place greater emphasis on high-value skills such as critical thinking, complex problem-solving, and creativity, while the importance of soft skills is moving to the center of the professional ecosystem. Although AI technologies deepen the existing gap between qualifications and labor market needs, they also provide powerful aids for personalized learning and competency development. Education systems that leverage data analytics and intelligent forecasting enable learners to acquire core competencies demanded by the future workplace more efficiently, accelerating the transition from foundational to advanced capabilities.

Qualifying for Tomorrow's Labor Market

Yet this technical advantage is unevenly distributed. Low-skilled workers bear the brunt of the negative impacts of the automation wave, and transitions reveal growing disparities among countries, industries, and even social strata. In a rapidly changing labor market, the unresolved question is how political support, industry collaboration, and technological innovation can be harnessed to bridge the gap between requirements and qualifications, a central challenge society must confront.

It is worth noting that in an AI-dominated economy, human uniqueness is not diminished but redefined. Demand for emotional intelligence (EI), communication skills, creativity, and social acumen is rising because these abilities have not yet been fully replicated or replaced by technology. Automation liberates individuals from repetitive work, creating space to focus on innovative and strategic tasks. EI, for instance, continues to prove indispensable in organizational leadership and complex decision-making.

The evolution of AI fosters a profound integration of human and machine capabilities, emphasizing each individual's ability to leverage personal strengths more effectively under technological support. Faced with this transformation wave, the promotion of comprehensive competency development becomes a central imperative. Industry leaders and policymakers must craft joint solutions to mitigate the social inequality caused by automation. Examples include flexible and effective learning platforms, financial support for reskilling, and social safety nets during transition phases.

Individuals must accept lifelong learning as the key rule for safeguarding employability. Only by balancing management skills, technological literacy, and emotional competencies, while continuously adapting to change, can people take a proactive role in the era of occupational transformation and ultimately maximize both individual and societal value.

As AI progresses, repetitive tasks are being replaced by intelligent systems at an astonishing pace. Simultaneously, the complexity and diversity of new tasks challenge human capabilities. How transformation and continuous development can occur on the fast-moving technological track will be central for individuals, companies, and society as a whole. The shift from low-value, repetitive work to high-value, demanding skills not only affects adaptability and competitiveness but also defines the role of labor in the global trend of digitalization.

Technological Displacement and the Loss of Traditional Jobs

AI is reshaping key industries with unprecedented force, delivering unreachable levels of efficiency while simultaneously causing deep disruption. Tasks that rely on repetitive, rule-based processes are increasingly being assumed by technological solutions, driving a rapid decline in the labor-market demand for traditional skills.

Manufacturing: The combination of machine vision systems and collaborative robots renders manual operations such as welding, assembly, or quality control almost redundant. Tesla's fully automated production line is a prime example: robots perform every core task.

Services: Powered by NLP technology, chatbots now operate at scale, handling vast volumes of user inquiries in seconds, from blocking lost bank cards to retrieving e-commerce logistics data, without any need for human customer service staff.

Finance and Office Work: Automation tools such as RPA memorize predefined rules and execute quantitative calculations, report generation, and data entry, replacing traditional data clerks and assistant analysts.

Although these technologies dramatically boost productivity and sharply reduce error rates, they also concentrate unemployment risk in low-skilled occupations. Companies that focus on technological optimization must systematically evaluate the impact of this displacement on their internal talent pools and develop appropriate transformation strategies.

The Rise of Peak Capabilities

Peak capabilities, characterized by innovation, sound judgment, and the mastery of complexity, are not constrained by repetitive tasks and remain difficult for AI to replicate. They are becoming indispensable core competencies in digital environments and demonstrate cross-industry universality.

Data-Driven Insight

AI can process vast data volumes efficiently, but extracting decisive information and translating it into strategy remains the domain of human expertise. In business processes, specialists with analytical skills secure decision quality through modeling, analysis, and visualization.

Example: A leading consumer goods firm used real-time consumption data to forecast demand, cut inventories, and reduced quarterly costs by 15%. The meticulous data analysis and algorithm refinement by its data scientists were critical.

Critical Thinking and Dynamic Problem-Solving

AI excels within clearly defined boundaries, yet reaches limits in complex, uncertain situations. Critical thinking and interdisciplinary integration are essential for tackling open-ended problems and unforeseen challenges. During sudden crises or unexpected political shifts, human leaders must rapidly evaluate alternatives, these are capabilities, algorithms cannot yet replace.

Innovation and Design Capabilities

Generative AI has made impressive strides in text and image creation. True innovation, like the opening of untapped markets or the design of groundbreaking business models, still depends on the creative flexibility of human thought. Innovative skills liberate individuals from traditional constraints and shape future trends.

Emotional Intelligence and Deep Empathy

Even when machines deliver near-perfect simulations, the subtle human-to-human interaction of specific emotional responses remains uniquely human. In medicine, education, and leadership, fields where psychological support is vital, the nuance of human interaction is irreplaceable.

Transformation Pathways and Practical Approaches

The future of peak capabilities depends not only on an individual's willingness to learn but also on systematic support from society, business, and government. This process requires collaboration among all stakeholders and a focus on the following five pillars:

Normalize Lifelong Learning

The rapid pace of technological change makes traditional "one-off" training obsolete. Lifelong learning is the foundation of what might be called "skill immunity."

Example: Companies can deploy "Learning-as-a-Service" (LaaS) platforms that allow employees to take modular courses and receive real-time feedback.

Foster Interdisciplinary and Versatile Talent

As AI accelerates industry convergence, cross-disciplinary knowledge is more critical than ever. The intersection of technology, business, and social issues demands generalists.

Example: A healthcare professional who also learns coding and algorithms can use wearable devices to deliver personalized diagnostics, which leads to dramatically increasing individual value.

Build Skills Through Real-World Problem-Solving

Learning must not be detached from context. Embedding genuine business challenges into training is the most natural way to cultivate capabilities.

Example: Internal innovation contests and pilot projects let employees systematically acquire the knowledge needed to solve actual problems.

Use AI to Accelerate Capability Leaps

Enterprises and educational institutions can leverage AI-based tools to diagnose individual weaknesses and dynamically optimize learning pathways, enabling truly personalized upskilling.

Example: Professional development software can recommend tailored courses and track progress in real time.

A Collaborative Vision for Comprehensive Capability Transformation

The rise of AI brings unique opportunities and urgent challenges. Capability building cannot rest on individual effort alone; it requires coordinated action among society, business, and government.

Businesses must treat capability reinvention as a long-term strategy, not a tactical fix.

Policymakers must open access to reskilling and transition programs to ensure socially sustainable workforce shifts.

The “gaps” left by technological displacement are not the end of employment. Upgrading traditional workers into peak-capability talent and integrating them with intelligent systems offers a chance to boost efficiency and redefine human agency.

1.9 Intelligent Adaptation of Learning Paths

In the context of globalization and accelerated technological change, adaptive learning has become a central need for social development. From basic education to lifelong learning, AI is revolutionizing the paradigm of education and training systems with its ability to process comprehensive data and make decisions, enabling a shift from the “one-size-fits-all” model to customized paths. In an era where knowledge is constantly being renewed at an ever-increasing pace, the question of how to design learning processes as efficiently as possible and promote continuous adaptability is at the forefront, a challenge that both individuals and organizations must face.

Artificial Intelligence Transforms Education and Professional Adaptability

The introduction of intelligent learning paths not only improves the precision of resource adaptation but also optimizes the learning experience and the transfer of professional competencies. In this section, we examine the potential and limitations of intelligent learning paths from the perspectives of technical principles, application scenarios, and implementation challenges, in order to offer readers inspiring approaches to thinking and practical solutions.

The Basic Concept of Intelligent Learning Paths

Traditional learning content and methods are based on collective design. In contrast, AI can generate dynamically adapted learning content and paths through a comprehensive analysis of the individual characteristics of learners. This change not only meets the need for flexible education in our fast-paced society but also redefines the logic of learning.

The development of intelligent learning paths is based on the following core principles:

Dynamic Adaptation and Feedback Optimization: Learning paths are monitored and adapted in real time by AI. For example, an individual feedback system based on learning progress enables the precise identification of weaknesses and offers corresponding practice units. This feedback loop transforms learning from a static to a dynamic process, thereby increasing the depth and speed of knowledge acquisition.

Integration of Skills at Different Levels: Intelligent learning paths promote the development of multidimensional competencies, from basic knowledge to complex application skills. For example, technical learners can work with both theoretical courses on algorithms and practice-oriented project modules, creating a closed loop between theory and application.

Forward-Looking Competence Development: Based on social, economic, and industrial trends, AI can predict future demands for skills. As a result, learners receive learning paths with future-oriented learning content to prevent "competence deficits" in the transfer of skills.

Technological Foundations

Data-Driven Intelligence and User Profiling

With the help of big data analytics technologies, a highly precise profile of a learner can be created, encompassing the respective knowledge level, learning behavior, interests, and goals. For example, the system can assess the learner's state and adjust the path accordingly by analyzing the time spent on tests, error rates, and preferred learning times.

The following optimization approaches can be mentioned here: Learners with high efficiency receive recommendations for challenging content and advanced requirements. When encountering learning blocks, suggestions for perspective shifts or practical examples for problem-solving are provided.

Natural Language Processing and Interaction Engines

NLP enables learners to interact directly with the intelligent system. An intelligent teaching assistant can address questions, create individual explanations, and identify knowledge gaps to suggest relevant content.

Typical functions here include understanding checks with concise explanations of complex theories. Automatic exercise generation is another aspect, offering tasks based on the learning level and promoting knowledge transfer.

Reinforcement Learning and Adaptive Optimization

Reinforcement learning algorithms enable continuous optimization of intelligent learning paths based on a learner's successes and feedback. Not only is the order of current learning modules adjusted, but the collected data also improves the overall system efficiency in the long term.

Support from Generative AI

Generative AI can create a variety of learning resources flexibly. For beginners, easy-to-understand materials are generated, while for advanced users, topics with innovative and complex approaches are prepared. This increases the efficiency of educational resource production and allows for their individual adaptation and scenario simulation (e.g., in virtual job interviews).

Outstanding Application Scenarios

Personalized Online Learning Platforms

Online platforms are the most suitable application field for intelligent learning paths. Platforms like Coursera use behavioral data to offer learners customized programs ranging from basic courses to certifications. With the help of knowledge graphs, these platforms identify the strengths and weaknesses of learners and provide tailored exercises.

Profession-Oriented Competence Development

The shortened innovation cycles in many industries demand continuous further education. Companies like Microsoft use AI-driven systems in their training programs to predict trends in areas such as cloud computing or data science and provide courses early on. The combination of personalized recommendations with practical case examples significantly accelerates the development of application-ready skills.

Adaptive Teaching Scenarios

Adaptive learning systems, often combined with Augmented Reality (AR), offer learners immersive educational environments. For example, surgical simulators in the medical field or flight simulators in aviation training provide practical experience with tasks whose difficulty level dynamically increases.

Key Questions in Implementation

Data and Ethical Risks

Creating personalized learning paths requires extensive user data, such as behavioral patterns and preferences. This poses significant privacy risks. It is crucial to maintain a balanced relationship between data-based optimization and user data protection.

Fairness and Universal Applicability

The effectiveness of intelligent learning paths largely depends on the diversity of training data. A lack of diversity in the data could lead to certain population groups being disadvantaged, further widening existing educational gaps.

New Roles for Teachers

With the spread of AI, the role of educators shifts from being a "knowledge transmitter" to a "mentor and supporter." How to design meaningful cooperation between teachers and AI while maintaining the human element in the educational process remains a central question in educational technology.

Conclusion: A Sustainable Transformation of Learning Through Technology

The intelligent adaptation of learning paths is not only a technological innovation but also a comprehensive revolution in educational forms and professional adaptability. AI makes educational resources more targeted and offers more efficient learning opportunities through dynamic optimization. However, this change requires increased attention to aspects such as fairness, ethical risks, and the human component in educational processes.

In the future, intelligent learning will not only enhance the professional adaptability of individuals but also contribute to creating more fairness and sustainability in educational structures. As pioneers in educational technology, it is our responsibility to work with technology to drive a significant and empathetic educational revolution.

1.10 Skills and Emotional Intelligence: The Complementary Effect

In the face of the powerful technology of AI, we are currently experiencing an unprecedented transformation. Many traditional skills are being replaced by automated algorithms, generative AI is showing the potential for iterative innovation, and data-model-driven precise decision-making is at the center of business processes. However, as tasks are handed over to machines, the question arises: Can humans still preserve their unique value in a technology-dominated world? The answer is increasingly focusing on emotional intelligence (EI), which is measured by EQ.

The Intersection of Technology and Emotions

EI, the ability to perceive and manage both one's own emotions and those of others, is becoming a central core competence in the age of AI. Although technologies can perform standardized tasks and optimize data-driven decisions, the ability to express emotions, show empathy, creativity, and engage in intercultural cooperation remains a deeply human asset that cannot be fully replaced at least in the foreseeable future. In this section, we examine the interface between technology and human capabilities from the perspective of EI. We analyze the future role of EQ, the complementary effect of technology and emotions, and their application in everyday life.

Rediscovering Human Values: The Role of Humans in Intelligent Collaboration

With the increasing integration of AI into various industries, a new ecosystem of skills has emerged. The focus on human values is shifting from mere mastery of technical skills to emphasizing human characteristics. The central dimensions of this shift are:

Emotional Competence That Machines Cannot Replicate: Affective AI can recognize emotions using technologies like speech processing and visual analysis but often falls short in contextualizing them. For example, AI can detect a worried facial expression but cannot determine whether it is due to stress, cultural differences, or long-term psychological strain. Fields such as psychological counseling, child-rearing, or patient care still require the nuanced perception and multidimensional thinking of humans.

The Development Path from "Technology" to "Emotions": As automation increasingly takes over tasks in data analysis, forecasting, and logical thinking, human competencies need to shift toward "emotion-driven" fields. This includes complex human interactions such as conflict management and emotion regulation in teams in dynamic environments. There is also a need for vision-driven leadership qualities. Inspired by emotional resonance and cultural sensitivity, these qualities should activate motivations and shape goals. Finally, ethical issues and social responsibility are crucial to analyze and balance the societal consequences of technological decisions.

The Model of Complementary Interaction Between Technology and EQ

The strength of AI lies in optimizing efficiency, while human EI endows efficiency with a valuable social dimension. Together, they can enable dynamic collaboration in the following areas:

Enhancing Efficiency in Human-Machine Collaboration

Building a robust complementary model of logical thinking (machine) and emotional action (human) can create a flexible and adaptive ecosystem of intelligent work.

Crisis management requires human-machine collaboration. Intelligent forecasting models can analyze target values in crisis situations, while leaders with high EI can manage team emotions. For example, a financial crisis can be better managed through a combination of AI-assisted analysis and human emotional regulation.

Human intuition combined with AI analysis is also needed. While AI provides technical analysis in areas such as medical diagnostics or strategic business planning, many decisions are based on emotional signals and human intuition to strategically balance variables.

Building a More Trustworthy Technological Environment

The rapid proliferation of AI is often accompanied by concerns about algorithmic transparency, data security, and ethics. Leaders with high EI can build trust among team members and external stakeholders.

By actively listening and communicating transparently, concerns or reservations about the use of AI among customers and the public can be alleviated. Within teams, openness can be promoted to strengthen trust in AI systems through collaborative decision-making.

Creative Problem-Solving for Complex Challenges

While AI can efficiently solve linear problems, it lacks the ability for non-linear thinking and emotional judgment. People with high EI can more effectively handle more uncertain scenarios. For example, they can build consensus through emotional identification in conflicts of interest, or creatively decipher vague needs that algorithms can hardly interpret and iterate technologically refined solutions.

Future Scenarios: Combining EQ and Technology

Practical case studies that combine EI with technological strategies have achieved success in various ways:

Intelligent Clinical Practice in Healthcare

An international hospital implemented an AI-assisted diagnostic system, significantly improving patient care efficiency. However, patients initially expressed concerns about the "dehumanization" of AI. Through adjustments, processes were designed so that AI handled data analysis, while empathetic doctors provided emotional support and explanations in personal conversations. This partnership of efficiency and emotional approach enhanced trust.

Emotional Innovation in Leadership Training

A multinational company used generative AI to analyze employees' technical data and individually adjust training rhythms based on identified emotional states. At the same time, virtual emotional simulators were integrated for leaders to train their empathy in stressful situations. This strategy increased efficiency by over 10% and improved team satisfaction.

Developing Emotional Intelligence in the Age of AI

To fully exploit the potential of AI while emphasizing human emotional strengths, there is a need for targeted development of the following competencies:

Emotion Recognition and Regulation

Through systematic training programs that include emotional analysis tools, people can learn to better interpret and regulate emotionally charged behavioral patterns.

Intercultural Communication Skills

Virtual reality tools can simulate global team scenarios to make nonverbal and emotional signals in intercultural projects understandable.

Ethical Sensitivity and Sense of Responsibility

Teams can be trained through ethical programs to critically question technological biases and social side effects and to develop balanced solutions.

Conclusion: Redefining the Boundaries Between Technology and Emotions

AI has revolutionized many traditional processes, but the targeted development of human EI makes the coexistence of humans and technology not only sustainable but also mutually beneficial.

The key to shaping the future lies in the balance between technical competence and EI. In a dynamic world, it is not only about integrating machines into human ecosystems but also ensuring through EI that technology serves the profound and diverse needs of humanity. This is a fundamental balancing act: technology is a tool for reality, while EI is the bridge to implementation.

Chapter 2
Application of AI in Companies

The rapid development of artificial intelligence (AI) is profoundly changing the rules and management techniques in companies. From simplifying processes to enhancing decision-making capabilities, its influence extends far beyond the boundaries of traditional management models. By integrating big data analytics and self-learning algorithms, AI not only achieves breakthroughs in areas such as efficiency and cost control but also shows remarkable progress in decision forecasting and strategic planning. However, the implementation of this technology comes with unique challenges, and companies must carefully consider these contradictions and potential impacts when promoting intelligent transformation. In operational management, AI demonstrates its added value particularly through cross-domain applications. Human resource management is a typical example. Intelligent recruitment systems use multidimensional data analysis and natural language processing (NLP) techniques to comprehensively evaluate the skills of applicants and their suitability for job profiles, thereby significantly increasing the precision and efficiency of the recruitment process. However, there is a risk that these algorithms may be influenced by biases in historical data, which could unintentionally exacerbate discrimination or create injustices. In the field of supply chain management, machine learning (ML)-based forecasting algorithms effectively optimize inventory and logistics models, but uncertainties in supply chains and incomplete data collection can still limit the reliability of the system. Therefore, companies must find a balance between flexibility and efficiency when introducing new technologies. In financial management, AI has also opened up entirely new perspectives. Automated auditing tools ensure financial compliance and help detect risks in real time through big data mining and anomaly detection. However, the high sensitivity of financial data poses special requirements for data protection and security. Companies must develop transparent frameworks that ensure both algorithmic transparency and data confidentiality. Moreover, while the automation of financial reporting by generative AI has significantly increased efficiency, it still cannot comprehensively cover complex in-depth analyses. This demands continuous professional development from financial experts. In production, AI has fundamentally transformed traditional industrial models through technologies such as machine inspection, predictive maintenance, and digital twins. The ability to monitor the condition of machines in real time and conduct simulations has significantly reduced downtime and costs and greatly improved production flexibility. However, flexible human-machine collaboration still requires overcoming bottlenecks in standardized processes. At the same time, implementing training for production workers and improving safety standards has become an indispensable aspect. The digitalization of marketing has opened up new ways for personalization and emotional analysis. AI-based personalized recommendations not only improve the customer experience but also significantly increase conversion rates. However, excessive

 | https://doi.org/10.1515/9783112242728-002

reliance on algorithms can weaken the market's innovation power and lead to the homogenization of services from different brands. Moreover, the sensitivity of emotion analysis algorithms to cultural and contextual nuances is difficult to fully achieve, which continues to limit their application in multilingual and multicultural markets. Although AI opens up new horizons for corporate activities, it could become a limitation for companies that do not strategically consider its use. This ranges from data biases to changes in qualification requirements, data protection issues, and technological dependence. Only when companies strive for a balance between technological advantages and ethical responsibility and establish dynamic learning and optimization mechanisms can they fully exploit the potential of AI. In the end, the true value of AI will not lie in the technology itself, but in its ability to strengthen the organizational ecosystem and society as a whole.

The widespread application of AI in the field of auditing and financial management fundamentally changes the logic of the industry. This transformation is based on the powerful data processing capabilities and precise analysis of complex problems by AI. In traditional auditing processes, human interventions and time-consuming manual tasks have limited efficiency and quality. With the introduction of AI, however, companies can deploy algorithms to quickly analyze large amounts of data, minimize human errors, and efficiently utilize resources. This not only simplifies cumbersome workflows but also provides executives with real-time scenarios and precise information for decision-making support, significantly enhancing the reliability and agility of corporate decisions. The rapid development of intelligent auditing technologies is a remarkable outcome in this area. AI models can identify automatic recognition patterns from unstructured data using ML and data mining techniques. They help companies detect potential risks and optimize auditing strategies. For example, risk-based monitoring tools based on deep learning can capture possible anomalies in transactions in real time, issue warnings, and provide efficient intervention recommendations for the financial management team. These forward-looking capabilities not only increase resource utilization but also enhance a company's resilient adaptability in complex compliance and risk scenarios. In the field of financial forecasting, AI breaks through traditional methodological boundaries. Based on deep learning algorithms and time series analysis, AI can extract significant patterns from historical data to provide more precise support for budget planning, cash flow management, and the optimization of investment portfolios. Particularly in an economically highly uncertain environment, AI-supported forecasting systems, with their higher sensitivity and objectivity, prove to be crucial in helping companies deal with market volatility and strategic adaptation. The effectiveness of this technology, however, depends on the coverage and quality of the training data, which significantly increases the requirements for data acquisition and cleaning. Moreover, AI shows enormous added value in the field of automated payment processes and expense reimbursement. With the help of anomaly detection and text analysis techniques, algorithms can automatically filter out suspicious travel expense claims or payment requests to prevent errors and fraud cases that can arise from manual inputs. The use of AI systems not only increases the depth of monitoring but also reshapes financial transparency and strengthens a company's compliance-oriented financial management structure. However, the sensitivity of different organizations to confidential data must be taken into account to find a balance between efficiency and data protection. Despite the many new possibilities that AI has opened up in auditing and the financial sector, companies face a variety of challenges when implementing this technology. On the one hand, the efficiency of AI models strongly depends on high-quality data, and inherent distortions in some analysis processes can limit application possibilities in complex environments. On the other hand, data security and data protection issues also pose a major hurdle for the introduction of AI technologies. In the face of increasingly stringent regulations, companies must pay more attention to compliance checks in technological implementation to comprehensively protect sensitive information and avoid potential reputational risks due to algorithmic distortions or improper use. At the interface of technology and ethics, companies must evaluate the use of AI from a strategic perspective at a higher level. The focus should not only be on short-term efficiency gains but also on long-term value creation and societal impacts. Only by finding the right balance between technological advantages and compliance requirements can companies sustainably utilize AI and draw lasting competitive advantages from the reshaping of auditing and financial management to remain successfully in a constantly changing economic environment.

2.1 Intelligent Auditing Through AI Audits

Auditing essentially involves the review and verification of data. The explosive growth of data in modern business environments, along with increased complexity, demands more efficient and precise auditing methods. With the development of AI, traditional person-centered sampling audits have evolved into AI-driven, more comprehensive and intelligent auditing methods. This transformation not only enhances the efficiency of auditing and the ability to detect risks but also redefines the role and boundaries of auditing to provide more strategic insights for businesses.

AI as a Driver in Auditing

The introduction of AI has revolutionized the auditing industry in several key aspects:

Expanded Data Scope: AI algorithms can process both unstructured and structured data, eliminating the selective biases of traditional sampling methods.

Real-Time Calculations and Dynamic Responses: Auditing has expanded from retrospective analysis to dynamic real-time monitoring.

Deep Pattern Recognition and Prediction: Complex ML models uncover deep data relationships, enabling the shift from anomaly detection to problem prediction.
Decision Support: AI automatically provides insights and action recommendations to support management in making data-driven decisions.

This is not just a technological upgrade but marks a paradigm shift in auditing practice. AI is no longer just a tool but the central innovation engine for reshaping processes.

Practical Application Examples of Intelligent Auditing

Comprehensive Data Processing and Risk Detection

In traditional audits, limited samples were relied upon due to the vast amounts and complexity of data. With AI, comprehensive data analysis can now be performed, achieving the following:

Integration of Heterogeneous Data Sources: AI can seamlessly integrate data from various formats and sources (financial reports, transaction logs, communication data) to ensure comprehensive coverage.
Precise Anomaly Detection: Using supervised and unsupervised learning algorithms, suspicious values can be identified and intelligently categorized, such as potential fraudulent transactions or erroneous bookings.
Multidimensional Analysis: By creating complex correlation diagrams, AI reveals interactions between different data and makes hidden risks visible.
Example: A large retailer uncovered several complex cases of financial fraud within its store network using AI-based multi-data analysis, preventing millions of euros in fraud.

Intelligent Risk Forecasting and Proactive Control

AI can not only identify existing problems but also simulate future risks to improve proactive risk management:

Behavioral Analysis for Data Forecasting: AI learns the specific behaviors of employees or departments from data and predicts potential risk scenarios, such as trends with a high likelihood of compliance violations.
Detection of External Dynamic Factors: By accessing real-time data on industry developments, regulatory changes, and market risks, AI can dynamically adjust audit priorities and weights.
Dynamic Alert Systems: Based on historical and ongoing operational data, AI automatically creates real-time alerts and suggests various solutions.

Example: A financial institution implemented an AI-supported model to predict credit behavior, immediately flagging potentially risky credit applications and reducing the rate of distressed loans by 15%.

Efficient Reporting and Insight Generation

Traditional audit reporting requires significant time for manual data and text processing. With the help of intelligent technologies, these processes are optimized:

Automated Models for Report Summaries: AI can extract audit summaries for specific processes or departments and highlight key areas such as business aspects and risk zones.

Multilingual Reporting Through Natural Language Processing: Particularly important for multinational companies, AI offers cross-language presentation of analyses.

Data Visualization: Through charts, heatmaps, and dynamic dashboards, AI visually presents important audit results and facilitates collaboration among different teams.

Example: A leading auditing firm reduced its reporting time from 10 days to 24 h using its AI-based audit assistant, while also improving the content quality and global coherence of the reports.

Advantages of Intelligent Auditing

The introduction of intelligent auditing brings significant benefits to the industry, including:

Comprehensive Auditing: Full data access allows for deeper verification and analysis, reducing errors that may occur through sampling methods.

Efficiency Improvement: AI tools handle time-consuming computational tasks in a fraction of the time of traditional methods.

Enhanced Insights: Through data interactions and deep learning, AI reveals trends that are difficult for human analysts to detect.

Increased Compliance and Transparency: Data-driven audits eliminate human influences, increasing the objectivity and traceability of results.

Example: A large energy supply company optimized its annual financial audit process using AI, increasing the detection rate of financial irregularities from 57% to 83%.

Challenges and Strategies How to Overcome Them

Despite the promising prospects, the practical application of intelligent auditing also faces challenges:

Complexity and Availability of Data: The standardization and integration of data from various processes directly affect the effectiveness of the models.

Solution: Use data cleaning tools and standardized data labeling techniques to improve data quality.
Interpretability and Trustworthiness: The "black box" problem of AI makes it difficult for auditors to explain the results of complex models.
Solution: Utilize interpretable AI technologies (e.g., SHAP and LIME) that provide clear causal relationships for the models.
Algorithmic Biases and Ethical Issues: Biases embedded in data can lead to unjustified erroneous judgments.
Solution: Carefully examine the fairness of input data and implement bias reduction strategies in the design of audit models.
Technology and Knowledge Gaps: The introduction of intelligent tools requires special skills that not all auditors possess.
Solution: Provide targeted training programs and develop platforms that promote interdisciplinary collaboration and knowledge sharing.

Perspective: The Expansion and Integration of Intelligent Auditing

With the further development of AI and its integration into other digital tools, intelligent auditing will be implemented comprehensively and its functions will be deepened:
AI Meets Blockchain: Through blockchain technology, the complete traceability of the auditing process is ensured, significantly increasing the reliability of results.
Self-Adapting Systems: Development of systems that automatically adjust rules and parameters to specific customer needs.
Expansion to Industry-Specific Collaboration: The joint use of AI models or big data technologies could open up access to intelligent auditing technologies for SMEs.
Transformation into a Complete Ecosystem: AI-driven audits will no longer be seen as an isolated tool, but as part of a comprehensive decision-making framework for management.
Example: An auditing firm is currently testing a holistic auditing solution that combines AI and blockchain to extend transparency and monitoring throughout the entire supply chain life cycle.

Conclusion

Intelligent auditing has evolved beyond mere technology into a strategic instrument that strengthens the resilience of a company and optimizes business logic. However, it is crucial not to overlook the associated challenges. The future of auditing will be determined not only by technological advancements but also by how well ethical and social norms can be aligned with this progress. Only through the integration of technological progress and social responsibility can the vision of a fair, efficient, and trustworthy new era of auditing be realized.

2.2 Financial Forecasting and Decision Support

In the context of intensifying global competition and accelerated market changes, financial management has evolved beyond traditional accounting and reporting functions to become a cornerstone of corporate governance. With the accelerated accumulation of available data and continuous technological progress, AI has triggered a comprehensive transformation in the financial sector. AI not only provides unparalleled insights and forecasting capabilities for financial teams but also offers organizations innovative solutions for resource allocation, risk management, and strategic expansion.

In this section, we analyze the key application scenarios of AI technology in financial forecasting and decision support. The scope ranges from data processing optimization to precise forecasting, risk assessment, and the development of investment strategies. Their practical value and limitations are comprehensively demonstrated to support businesses in unlocking future potential in financial management.

Data Integration and Intelligent Preprocessing

One of the most critical foundational tasks in financial management is the collection, cleaning, and integration of heterogeneous data from various sources. Traditional methods often reach their limits when dealing with issues such as incomplete data, data silos, and redundant repetitions, which can affect the accuracy of analysis results. The contribution of AI in this area is particularly noteworthy:

Data Cleaning and Standardization: Using ML algorithms, AI tools can quickly identify and fix missing values, outliers, and duplicate entries in data to maintain stable data quality. For example, the financial industry has significantly reduced the time-consuming manual data cleaning process by employing deep learning models to process large amounts of historical transaction data – to 30% of the effort.

Automated Data Integration: AI systems can extract data from ERP, CRM, and financial management software and store it in a unified standard format, enabling data integration across different systems. This standardization capability has greatly optimized accounting and consolidation processes, especially in multinational corporations.

By efficiently cleaning and integrating data, AI raises the accuracy and interpretability of financial analyses to a new level and creates a solid foundation for subsequent forecasting models.

Enhanced Forecasting and Dynamic Modeling

Traditional financial forecasts are based on human experience and limited statistical models. In a complex and constantly changing market environment, these methods are often slow and inflexible. AI overcomes these limitations through self-learning models and real-time dynamic modeling, offering businesses entirely new forecasting tools.

Intelligent Revenue Forecasting

AI uses time-series analysis algorithms and regression models to train on historical corporate data while incorporating external variables (such as industry trends, market forecasts, and political dynamics) in real time. Examples include:

Identifying Individual Demand Patterns: A retail company used AI to capture consumer preferences and the impact of holidays, creating a precise sales forecasting model. This led to optimized inventory levels and a 30% reduction in inventory holding costs, as shown in industry-specific reports.

Early Warning for Unusual Growth: AI systems can detect sales changes outside historical patterns and provide early warnings of potential market events or issues, giving corporate leadership sufficient time to react.

Dynamic Budgeting

Traditional static budgets, based on last year's data, are often not flexible enough to respond to real-time changes. AI breaks this limitation with its ability to optimize the budgeting process in real time:

Automatic Variable Adjustment: AI tools can dynamically adjust budget modules based on historical departmental budgets, market developments, or external influencing factors (such as fluctuations in raw material prices).

Scenario Simulation: Using AI techniques for "hypothesis testing," companies can simulate several possible scenarios, such as a 10% cost increase or a 15% market share loss, to prepare financial adjustments for potential changes.

Case Study: Implementation of a Dynamic Budgeting Mechanism

A large manufacturing company launched a pilot project for dynamic budget management on an AI-supported platform. The platform conducted several predictive adjustment cycles: When fluctuations in raw material prices exceeded a certain threshold, the model immediately optimized the budget allocation and simultaneously proposed new procurement processes. This not only prevented resource wastage but also significantly enhanced cross-departmental collaboration efficiency, marking the transition from static budgeting to dynamic resource allocation.

Risk Analysis and Automated Management

Risk management is a core component of financial decision support. AI improves the accuracy of risk analyses by enabling real-time interaction between internal financial data and external market indicators, allowing companies to build proactive risk management systems.

Credit Risk Modeling

In terms of credit risk associated with loans and business relationships, AI models generate precise default forecasts by analyzing historical repayment habits, large transaction records, and deviations in credit ratings. Financial institutions and small and medium-sized enterprises (SMEs) along the supply chain have successfully implemented this in practice: A European financial firm used AI models to monitor risks post-credit issuance and identified 12% of potentially high-risk customers early on, thereby reducing daily capital losses by 8%.

Macro-risk Insights

AI is not limited to risk management within a company but also uses NLP to analyze political messages, news, and social media comments to generate early warnings for external environmental changes. For example, the finance team of a multinational company deployed an AI risk system that tracked changes in trade policies and global supply chain disruptions in real time. The system adjusted 20% of the financing direction for a planned overseas investment, thereby avoiding potential significant losses.

Optimization of Investment and Strategic Models

Compared to the often cumbersome and data-intensive processes in investment decision-making, AI enables companies to adapt strategically in a flexible and dynamic manner, thereby more efficiently allocating capital.

Asset Allocation and Market Intelligence

By analyzing the fluctuations and correlations of different investment types, AI algorithms can design diversified investment portfolios that minimize risk. A leading fund management company used an AI platform based on market data to adjust the portfolio composition daily, thereby increasing returns and reducing the variance of investment returns by 40%.

Identification of New Market Opportunities

Many companies use AI to identify potential, untapped markets. For example, a US start-up used a generative AI analysis tool to quickly discover the growth needs in the online education sector in Southeast Asia. As a result, an expansion originally planned for 6 months was launched within 2 months. Such insights provide companies with speed advantages in their development strategies that are difficult to achieve through other means.

Challenges and Sustainable Implementation

Despite the impressive potential of AI in financial forecasting and decision support, there are still technical and non-technical challenges in widespread application:

- Algorithm Transparency: Some AI tools have a “black box” effect, causing financial executives to be skeptical of the results. The solution lies in introducing explainable AI (XAI) to make the model logic traceable.
- Data Privacy and Ethics: The sensitivity of financial data and regional legal differences require strict technical and regulatory-compliant measures when implementing AI systems.
- Cost of Organizational Change: Traditional finance teams often struggle to adapt to AI-driven analytical models. Companies should bridge the capability gap by providing targeted training and recruiting interdisciplinary fintech experts.

Outlook: From Support Tool to Empowering Technology

In the next phase of development, AI will be more deeply integrated into financial systems. By combining generative AI, deep learning approaches, and blockchain technology, companies may achieve the following in the future:

- Real-Time Generation of Investment Strategy Recommendations: AI will no longer just provide data results but also action guidelines, such as “Reduce the marketing budget by 10% and invest in supply chain optimization.”

Financial Ecosystem Collaboration: AI will create a closed loop through Internet of Things (IoT) data and information flows from partner companies, promoting a more tightly integrated decision-making framework.

Financial management is entering an intelligent era that considers technology as a core driving force. Companies should focus on long-term strategic planning when deploying AI and view innovation as a key component of competitiveness. With the use of human-machine collaboration, future financial decision-making will no longer be merely data-driven but will be full of strategic vision and intelligence.

2.3 Automated Payments: The Revolution of Financial Transparency

In the face of the growing corporate demand for increased efficiency and financial transparency, traditional payment and reimbursement management is increasingly confronted with challenging conditions. As a transformative technology, AI has already established itself in this field and offers novel approaches to process optimization and risk management. From intelligent auditing to dynamic payment optimization, AI is driving financial administration from labor-intensive individual checks to intelligent real-time solutions. This transformation not only addresses traditional problems but also paves the way for more efficient and structured management systems.

Challenges: Bottlenecks and Error Risks in Traditional Payment and Reimbursement Management

Payment and reimbursement management has always been characterized by the following fundamental issues:

Complex Processes and Low Efficiency: Manual data entry, approvals, and checks consume a lot of time and resources, especially in large companies.

Lack of Accuracy and Compliance: Erroneous data, duplicate reimbursements, and non-compliant transactions are often insufficiently monitored and pose financial risks.

Lack of Transparency: Decentralized processes and isolated information silos make it difficult for management to gain clear insights into expenditures.

These problems are particularly noticeable in companies with high activity and large transaction volumes. Here, the integration of AI technology offers effective solutions.

AI-Supported Processes for Payments and Reimbursements

AI is used in the automation of payments and reimbursements in various ways to improve processes and reduce administrative costs. It also enables automated compliance checks.

Intelligent Data Auditing and Anomaly Detection

Modern AI algorithms automatically flag suspicious entries in reimbursement data and significantly increase the accuracy of audits. Core technologies include classification algorithms that identify duplicate reimbursement requests, clustering models that detect unusual amounts or irregular frequencies, and predictive models that generate alerts for audits.

Practical Example: A government agency implemented an AI-supported reimbursement system and found that 20% of reimbursement anomalies were due to duplicate submissions. Three months after the introduction, this figure dropped to below 2%.

Real-Time Compliance and Automated Policy Application

Using NLP, corporate policies are analyzed and dynamically embedded in audit frameworks to ensure that each reimbursement meets the established standards. Innovative technologies with policy alignment modules help. These are based on predefined policies and real-time updates and generate systematic alerts for excessive spending or unauthorized expense types. The results and positive impacts were observed in a test phase. For example, AI-based auditing increased the match rate of policy applications at a financial institution to 98% and minimized delays caused by human misjudgments.

Dynamic Payment Optimization

Optimization algorithms create dynamic payment scenarios by analyzing transaction amounts, priorities, and fund availability, which stabilizes financial liquidity. The technological architecture includes a dynamic payment system that, combined with real-time data of pooled funds, creates priorities for the reimbursement queue and implements adaptive rules for intelligent payment sequencing. A multinational company improved its departmental capacity to process over 9,000 transactions per month with this solution, compared to 5,000 previously. The reimbursement duration was shortened by 37%.

User-Friendliness Through Intelligent Interaction and Optimized User Experience

AI systems also offer chatbots and voice assistants to help employees with complex reimbursement requests, reducing operational hurdles. The interaction design was conceived so that conversational AI guides users through the application, immediately flags erroneous data, and reduces the need for additional communication between employees and finance staff. A large retail company reported efficiency gains, with the introduction of an intelligent reimbursement application reducing the number of complaints by 43%.

Example: Implementation of an Automated Payment Platform at a Manufacturing Company

A regional manufacturing company implemented an AI-supported automated payment platform to address efficiency issues and fragmented data in the traditional reimbursement process. The results showed that automated auditing reliably reduces risks. The AI identified duplicate cost positions and corrected reimbursements that exceeded the budget, thereby avoiding overpayments. Payment processes were also optimized. Reimbursement payments were automatically processed through intelligent sequencing algorithms, effectively preventing liquidity bottlenecks in the central pool. Finally, transparent reports were automatically generated. The platform provided real-time dynamic reports, which significantly improved decision-making at the management level. According to analysis, the efficiency of the company's financial operations increased by 40%, while the risk of non-compliance was reduced by 80%.

Limitations and Challenges: Bottlenecks in Technology Implementation

Despite the significant improvements brought by AI in payments and reimbursements, there are still some hurdles in implementation:

Dependency on Data Quality: The effectiveness of AI algorithms depends on high-quality data, but many companies have significant shortcomings in historical financial data, which naturally affects model performance.

Technical Errors and Biases: Some anomaly detection algorithms may overlook specific scenarios or trigger false alarms, increasing the workload for audit staff.

Cultural Adaptation: Reimbursement formats and policies vary greatly between companies and countries – AI systems need time to adapt to different cultural contexts.

Future Outlook: Development Paths of Intelligent Payment and Reimbursement Processes

With advancing technology and growing corporate demands, the following trends can be identified for AI-based payment and reimbursement systems:

Fully Autonomous Audits and Payments: Human influence will be further reduced, and reimbursement systems will be able to automate audits and payments completely.
Integration of Multiple Business Areas: AI systems will be seamlessly connected with ERP systems, budget management solutions, and external audit software to create an integrated platform.
Enhanced Data Privacy Management: Data encryption and anonymization will become standard features of payment systems to meet strict financial data protection requirements.
Extended Analysis and Forecasting Capabilities: Finance departments will be able to predict the entire cash flow behavior of the company through reimbursement data to support strategic decisions.

Conclusion and Suggestions

AI is highly suitable for optimizing processes and reducing risks in payment systems and reimbursements. Despite existing technical and application-related challenges, the advantages in terms of efficiency gains, risk reduction, and improved transparency are already clearly visible. Companies that can combine innovative technologies with data security and employee training will better implement the intelligent transformation of financial management and pave the way for a more efficient, transparent, and compliant organization.

2.4 Industry 4.0, Production, and Machine Vision

The manufacturing industry is in the midst of a profound transformation driven by AI. Traditional production models are increasingly evolving toward digitalization and intelligence. This shift not only enhances production efficiency but also creates more flexible and sustainable operational models that can better and more quickly meet the diverse needs of consumers. With the help of AI, the manufacturing industry is moving from large-scale centralized production methods to personalized and customized services, thereby redefining the future of the sector. The optimization of production processes has become a key focus of intelligent manufacturing. Technologies such as machine vision and deep learning enable significant improvements in precision and efficiency through real-time monitoring and quality control, while also reducing labor costs and human errors. This transformation marks the transition from local optimization to holistic optimization and lays the foundation for the automation of complex production processes.

The AI-driven data-centric “smart factory” represents a highly interconnected production environment that will play a central role in the future of the manufacturing industry. In such networks, data application permeates all areas, from equipment monitoring to workforce scheduling and decision-making, thereby fundamentally enhancing operational efficiency and system transparency. However, this technological innovation also brings with it numerous challenges. Data privacy and security issues are becoming increasingly prominent, especially in the highly data-dependent environment of smart factories, where security vulnerabilities could lead to significant economic consequences. Meanwhile, the complexity of technological integration poses high demands on existing production systems, especially in terms of modernizing traditional facilities and coordinating diverse technologies. In addition, technological changes require new qualification standards for employees, making retraining and knowledge transfer key elements. This process is not only crucial for the implementation of technology but also a central point of conflict in the ecosystem of intelligent manufacturing. Under the leadership of AI, the manufacturing industry not only achieves efficiency improvements and intelligence in production processes but also develops comprehensive optimization capabilities in areas such as product development and market response. This systematic and continuous improvement helps to enhance the competitiveness of manufacturing companies and drives the entire industry toward data-driven and technology-based innovation. In this context, the intelligent transformation of the manufacturing industry not only promotes economic efficiency but also plays an increasingly important role in the global industrial competitive landscape.

The Integration of Machine Vision and Industrial Revolution

The wave of Industry 4.0 has initiated a comprehensive transformation in the manufacturing industry driven by technology. In this transformation process, machine vision is regarded as a core technology because it is deeply integrated with AI and image processing capabilities, thereby providing a solid foundation for the revolutionization of production efficiency, quality control, and operational models. Through real-time data acquisition, precise analysis, and intelligent decision-making, machine vision is driving the manufacturing industry toward automation and intelligence enhancement.

This section focuses on the application logic of machine vision in the context of Industry 4.0 and examines in detail the underlying technical principles, key applications, as well as the challenges and development trends that are leading the manufacturing industry toward an efficient production ecosystem.

Technical Principles: The Functional Logic of Machine Vision

Machine vision systems are technologies that imitate and surpass human visual capabilities to capture, process, and analyze image information. Their components include hardware sensors, optical devices, control electronics with software, and intelligent algorithms. The way they work can be outlined as follows:

High-Precision Image Capture: The manufacturing industry's demand for visual information is characterized by high precision and stability. With the help of industrial cameras and adjustable light sources, machine vision systems can capture detailed images even under extreme environmental conditions. Infrared light sources or multispectral cameras are typical solutions for capturing images in low-light environments.

Intelligent Image Analysis: By combining deep learning with traditional image processing algorithms, machine vision has powerful recognition capabilities. For example, convolutional neural networks are widely used for the classification and recognition of complex patterns, while transfer learning improves the adaptability of models when there is a limited amount of data.

Real-Time Automated Control: The system processes the analysis results of images into logical commands (such as classification control and error detection). The dynamic learning mechanism of AI endows the system with high adaptability, which is particularly advantageous in an environment where a mix of different products is being produced.

Application Scenario 1: Quality Control and Product Optimization

Improving Quality and Production Efficiency

Traditional quality control is susceptible to subjective errors due to manual handling and inspection. Particularly with diverse requirements, adapting inspection criteria poses a challenge. Machine vision brings high precision and consistency to quality control through high-resolution image recognition and automated processing.

In an application example, an electronics company implemented a multichannel vision system for comprehensive inspection of microelectronic components. Soldering points and dimensional deviations were detected within milliseconds, and future potential risks in the manufacturing process were predicted based on historical data. This system reduced the failure rate to below 0.1% and accelerated delivery times.

Providing Closed-Loop Data Flows

Data generated by machine vision is used not only for ongoing quality control but also for optimizing production line design. For example, analyzing error distributions and trends over the past 6 months helped a factory identify bottlenecks and improve utilization rates.

Application Scenario 2: Automated Sorting and Supply Chain Optimization

Increasing Sorting Efficiency and Cost Reduction

In manufacturing and logistics processes, machine vision is the key to automated sorting solutions. Through intelligent recognition (pattern recognition) of shape, color, and material structure, the system can quickly sort objects and ensure a fully automated process.

A globally operating food processing company, for example, uses a robot sorting system based on machine vision to recognize 300 different types of fruits and vegetables. This system decides on ripeness and compliance within milliseconds and removes unusable products. Operational efficiency is six times higher than manual sorting, saving the company millions of euros in operating costs annually and reducing waste.

Collaborative Robots Lead the Logistics Revolution

Machine vision and industrial robots have transformed traditional warehousing and logistics systems into intelligent delivery networks. For example, the automated warehouses of an e-commerce giant use visual systems to recognize shelf heights and object shapes to determine optimal transportation routes. This system significantly reduces delivery times, eliminates any manual interaction in the ordering process, and enables multitasking.

Application Scenario 3: Equipment Monitoring and Proactive Maintenance

Real-Time Monitoring to Minimize Downtime

Machine vision overcomes the limitations of traditional, cyclical maintenance methods and enables predictive error detection in real time. For example, camera and AI systems in critical areas of machines can detect anomalies such as wear, temperature increases, or unusual vibrations. Such warnings reduce the risk of unexpected equipment failures and associated losses.

Strengthening the Entire Production System

By visually monitoring equipment performance, production lines can be maintained more efficiently. This strategy goes beyond solving individual equipment problems and optimizes the overall system state. A leading automobile manufacturer implemented visual maintenance to ensure 24/7 monitoring, significantly reducing delivery delays caused by equipment failures.

Current Challenges and Implementation Issues

Lack of Adaptability to Extreme Environments

Machine vision performs excellently under stable conditions but reaches its limits in extreme environments such as heat, humidity, or obscured scenarios. This limitation can affect the efficiency of the technology in special processes and under harsh conditions.

High Implementation Costs

Integrating hardware and optimizing algorithms is complex, causing small and medium-sized enterprises to struggle with high investment and maintenance costs. The high upfront costs reduce the general spread of the technology.

Data Security and Privacy Risks

In the interconnected environments of Industry 4.0, manufacturing data becomes a central asset of a company. How to protect these visual operational data from cyberattacks is a crucial aspect of industrial development.

Skill Shortage

Operating and maintaining machine vision systems requires specialized skills. The current shortage of qualified personnel hinders both complexity reduction and overall progress in technology acceptance.

Future Outlook: An Evolving Intelligent Ecosystem

With the deep integration of machine vision in quality assurance, edge computing, and high-performance sensors, the application areas of this technology will continue to expand. Especially in smart factories, machine vision will increasingly drive holistic optimization in the manufacturing industry.

In the future, reducing technology costs and increasing algorithm adaptability will be key factors. With technological progress, social support, and growing market demand, lowering entry barriers will enable more companies to use this technology to transform the manufacturing industry beyond efficiency optimization into a resilient and flexible intelligent ecosystem.

Concluding Thoughts and Strategic Considerations

The importance of machine vision is not only in improving production efficiency and precision but also in profoundly influencing the business models and industrial ecosystem of the manufacturing industry. Machine vision is not only a technical tool for factory operations but also a window that improves the framework and trends of the Industry 4.0 era.

To achieve comprehensive implementation of machine vision, it is important to find a balance between technology and cost as well as between efficiency and resilience. At the same time, sustainable industrial ecosystems should be created through talent development and security strategies. This change marks not only a milestone for the technological upgrading of the manufacturing industry but also opens up new possibilities for collaboration between machine vision and other future technologies.

2.5 Digital Twins and Predictive Maintenance

In the context of modern industrial transformation, digital technologies are driving progress in mechanical engineering, product and production planning, and corresponding asset management. The digital twin, with its ability to combine physical and virtual worlds, has become a core tool for increasing industrial efficiency and optimizing resource use. The digital twin changes the traditional approach of reactive maintenance, enabling companies to anticipate potential risks in operations. This not only enhances production flexibility and reduces costs but also unleashes previously untapped potential. This section comprehensively analyzes the technical foundations, application scenarios, and future prospects of the digital twin, as well as the new era of predictive maintenance it ushers in.

What Is a Digital Twin?

A digital twin is a data-driven virtual model created through real-time data collection of physical devices or systems. It serves not only as a “mirror image” of the physical system but also provides a detailed representation of the capabilities, status, and behavior of equipment, machines, and devices. By integrating virtual and physical worlds, companies can monitor the status of devices in real time, optimize operational efficiency, and conduct risk-free experiments in virtual environments to avoid costly mistakes.

Example: A large wind power company can create digital twins for its operational wind turbines and perform holistic simulations and adjustments of weather conditions, load changes, and system states. With this system, they identified optimal configuration parameters under dozens of operational scenarios and increased energy efficiency by more than 15%.

Key Features and Functions of the Digital Twin

As a key component of Industry 4.0, the digital twin is the result of combining various technologies. Its functionality is extremely diverse. The key features include:

Bidirectional Data Interaction: The digital twin forms a closed data connection between the physical and virtual worlds through the collaboration of IoT sensors, edge computing, and cloud computing technologies. The status of the physical system or connected physical systems is reflected in real time in the virtual model, while instructions from model optimization can quickly impact the physical devices.

Real-Time Capability: Digital twins capture and analyze dynamic data in milliseconds. This ensures that every critical monitoring point can respond quickly to support predictions.

Life Cycle Coverage: From design, development, and manufacturing to operation and maintenance, the digital twin accompanies the entire life cycle of a device or system and provides decision-making foundations through in-depth data analysis.

Precise Modeling and Simulation: Using 3D modeling and physical simulation algorithms, digital twins can precisely replicate the internal workings of complex systems and the effects of external influences.

How the Digital Twin Enables Predictive Maintenance

Traditional industrial maintenance concepts have developed slowly since the Industrial Revolution and still mainly rely on reactive approaches or time-based schedules. These methods are inefficient and costly in the context of complex systems. The digital twin completely redefines the maintenance process through predictive approaches. The key components are:

Anomaly Detection and Warning: Digital twins identify potential anomalies through big data analysis and comparison of desired and actual device states. For example, a slight increase in noise levels in the storage of high-precision machines can trigger a warning. This allows the maintenance team to prepare resources for repair or replacement and prevents machine failure or, in the worst case, complete shutdown.

Intelligent Diagnosis and Root Cause Analysis: After a warning, the digital twin not only shows the problem but also identifies the exact cause using data analysis and algorithms. For example, if an industrial robot production line shows a decrease in efficiency, the digital twin can trace the cause back to a faulty material sensor instead of mistakenly assuming a system design flaw.

Dynamic Adjustment and Operational Optimization: Thanks to digital twins, predictive maintenance is not limited to repair and maintenance processes but also includes production planning. For example, a steel mill uses digital twins to optimize the production cycle of its blast furnaces. By predicting the lifespan of critical components, it can adjust the shift schedule to maximize production capacity while ensuring a seamless maintenance process.

Application Examples

The predictive maintenance capabilities of digital twins have been proven in various industries and have opened up new operational models and value creation spaces.

Manufacturing Industry: In the field of high-precision CNC machines, digital twins monitor the status of cutting tools and spindles in real time, reducing downtime caused by sudden equipment failures. At the same time, multiple configuration parameters can be tested in virtual simulations to ensure that machines operate in their optimal performance range. This ensures availability, reduces production costs, and improves product quality.

Energy Industry: The operation and maintenance costs of wind turbines or gas turbines are enormous. A failure leads directly to energy loss. Digital twins allow energy companies to monitor every parameter precisely and predict the best maintenance time according to lifespan models. This avoids errors in manual inspections and reduces the cost of replacing components.

Logistics and Warehousing: In modern automated warehouses, AGV systems (Automated Guided Vehicles) are constantly under stress. Digital twins monitor the wear rates of tires and batteries to predict the appropriate maintenance time and avoid failures. Additionally, the overall layout simulation of the warehouse can help optimize transportation routes.

Implementation Challenges

Despite the strong impetus that digital twins and predictive maintenance provide for industrial optimization, there are still some barriers in implementation:

High Implementation Costs: Small and medium-sized enterprises often cannot afford the purchase of sensors, model development, and the construction of algorithms for digital twins.

Complexity of Integration Services: The different data standards and heterogeneous equipment and systems in factories make the rapid and comprehensive integration of digital twins difficult.

Data Security Risks: Since digital twins rely heavily on cloud computing to process sensitive data, security vulnerabilities are potentially vulnerable to hacker attacks or data leaks.

Lack of Professional Talent: Implementing and maintaining digital twin systems requires multidisciplinary talents, but such talents are currently limited on the market.

Future Perspectives

Networking and Intelligence Upgrades

In the future, the digital twin will expand from the device level to broader system-wide applications, creating an intelligent, networked factory operation system. This will significantly enhance resource coordination across the entire production and value chain, extending to the supply chain, and make industrial decision-making smarter and more sustainable.

Deeper Integration with Artificial Intelligence

When combined with generative AI, digital twins can not only suggest optimal decisions but also generate creative and valuable maintenance strategies in real time. For example, in the event of further equipment failures, optional repair strategies can be developed and evaluated to shorten response times.

Decentralized Architectures

Advancements in edge computing open new possibilities for digital twins. Decentralized architectures enable factories to efficiently analyze critical local data while complex global optimization tasks continue to be handled by central cloud systems.

Conclusion

The emergence of digital twins marks a paradigm shift from "static management" to "dynamic collaboration" in industrial production. As a key technology with modern predictive maintenance, it not only meets the requirements of industrial automation but also forms the basis for future-oriented intelligent decision-making. In this data-driven era, companies need not only technological investments but also strategic thinking to combine visionary characteristics with integration capabilities.

The introduction of digital twins further enhances forecasting capabilities. Through dynamic data interaction between virtual and real systems, companies can gain in-depth insights and evolve their production activities from reactive repairs to real-time predictions and proactive optimization. This significantly reduces downtime and maintenance costs.

2.6 Human-Machine Collaboration: Building Flexible Capabilities

In an era of intensified global competition and increasingly differentiated consumer needs, the manufacturing industry is in the midst of a transition from large-scale assembly line production to highly flexible and customized production models. However, this shift also brings challenges regarding production efficiency, flexibility, and resource allocation. As a key technology of the digital transformation, human-machine collaboration combines intelligent devices with human creativity, enabling iterative improvements in production methods through collaborative robots and workforce.

Human-Machine Collaboration in Intelligent Manufacturing

This section explores the technological integration, characteristics, and far-reaching impact of human-machine collaboration on the industry.

Core Features of Human-Machine Collaboration

High Flexibility: From Rigid Automation to Dynamic Adaptation

Traditional automation systems are often fixed on predefined processes and respond inadequately to market changes or customized requirements. In contrast, human-machine collaboration systems support the transition from rigid production automation to flexible manufacturing strategies through intelligent algorithms and data-driven control. For example, in custom furniture manufacturing, collaborative robots can adjust to individual design requirements without causing long production downtimes for tool changes or programming modifications. This dynamic adaptability allows companies to flexibly allocate tasks and adjust production capacities under uncertain conditions such as fluctuating raw material supply or increasing demand for specific skills, achieving optimal resource utilization.

Balancing Innovation and Safety: Building a “Trustworthy” Collaboration Environment

In the past, industrial robots operated in isolated, separate areas to ensure workplace safety. Human-machine collaboration breaks these physical boundaries. Collaborative robots can perceive and predict the behavior of objects and people in the working environment to avoid collisions and dangerous processes through integrated embedded sensors, force feedback mechanisms, and real-time monitoring capabilities. For example, an alarm is triggered or work execution is stopped when the minimum distance between the robot and a human is violated. This balance not only avoids the traditional expensive protective barriers but also significantly improves the efficiency of human-machine interaction.

Data Analytics as a Value Driver

In flexible production, data serves not only as the basis for operational execution but also as the key to intelligent optimization. Through IoT sensors and cloud integration, collaborative devices can obtain real-time data on machine performance, production cycles, and environmental parameters, which are analyzed by AI algorithms to generate optimization suggestions. For example, based on the analysis of deviations in production lines, problems can be identified in advance and production planning can be adjusted to avoid delays or quality risks. The shift from reactive to predictive data-driven collaboration enables companies to increase efficiency while achieving long-term value growth.

Platforms for Successful Human-Machine Collaboration

Collaborative Robots (Cobots): Technological Breakthroughs and Application Expansion

As the core hardware of human-machine collaboration, collaborative robots (cobots) are characterized by their lightweight structure, flexible operability, and interactive user-friendliness. From the assembly of electronic products to food processing, cobots demonstrate their unique strengths in highly repetitive work scenarios. For example, the UR series from Universal Robots has shown its capabilities in the manufacturing of medical devices by sorting high-precision parts and achieving an error rate of less than 10 ppm.

Recent technological advancements also enable these robots to map environmental features: By combining computer vision and tactile feedback, they can adapt to the material properties of different surfaces. Therefore, even in constantly changing production conditions or less optimized workshops, they can perform tasks precisely and significantly simplify the system integration process.

Human-Machine Interaction Technologies: Enabling "Seamless" Collaboration

Seamless real-time communication between humans and machines is the foundation for the efficient execution of collaborative technologies. Through NLP, speech, and gesture recognition, workers can flexibly control robots with voice or gesture commands. For example, logistics workers can directly state the part number of the required component, and the robot will retrieve it and bring it to the specified location without manual data entry.

In addition, augmented reality (AR) technology enhances the user-friendliness and efficiency of collaboration with cobots. AR glasses can display optimal work steps and adjustment tips in complex working environments and simultaneously guide the robot to execute the pending tasks synchronously and efficiently.

Dynamic Planning and Edge Computing: Enhancing Real-Time Responsiveness

Compared with traditional centralized production systems, human-machine collaborative solutions are often based on dynamic decentralized planning models. Edge computing enables local data processing and rapid responsiveness by delegating decision-making authority directly to the workshop, thereby optimizing locally collected data and accelerating the decision-making process. Therefore, when sudden disturbances such as machine failures occur, the production line can quickly redistribute the corresponding tasks to avoid production downtime.

Application Cases: Extensive Practice of Flexible Production

Personalized Production of Electronic Products

A well-known electronics manufacturer employs human-machine collaboration to transition entirely from traditional mass production to personalized manufacturing. Collaborative robots take on tasks such as printed circuit board wiring and soldering with high efficiency, while human workers can dynamically adjust the specific product design, such as reconfiguring the front panel interfaces. This system reduces the production time for small batches by 45% and simultaneously enhances adaptability to market demands.

Adaptive Order Picking in Intelligent Warehouse Logistics

The logistics service provider JD Logistics has introduced an order-picking system based on human-machine collaboration, where robots retrieve goods from warehouse shelves and bring them close to the worker. Workers can thus complete the order-picking process entirely without leaving their workstation. This human-machine division of labor model increases efficiency per order and simultaneously reduces the physical strain on workers.

High-Precision Component Assembly in the Aerospace Industry

The aerospace industry demands the highest precision in connecting and aligning components to ensure flight safety and material reliability. In an aircraft assembly plant, a human-machine collaboration system, with the help of collaborative robots, performs 85% of repetitive assembly processes, allowing human workers to focus on the calibration and control of critical components. This reduces the overall error rate in production to 0.1%.

Future Trends and Central Conflicts of Human-Machine Collaboration

Trend: Multidimensional Role Restructuring and Full Collaboration

In the future, human-machine collaboration will increasingly be integrated into design, quality control, and operational management, moving beyond production. Collaborative systems will no longer perform only predefined tasks but will increasingly shape and optimize more complex value chains, leading to a new “human-machine dual-role model.”

Trend: Deeper Penetration into Vertical Industries

With the increasing adaptability and cost reduction of collaborative robots, their use will expand from the manufacturing industry to areas such as healthcare, education, and services. For example, collaborative robots could in the future support surgeries in medicine, prepare instruments, and provide real-time image navigation, significantly enhancing the quality of medical care.

Conflict: Nonlinear Balance Between Costs and Benefits

Despite a decrease of over 30% in the acquisition costs of entry-level devices, the follow-up costs for infrastructure upgrades and data security management remain a significant challenge for companies. Moreover, the widely varying requirements of different industries complicate the introduction of universally applicable solutions.

Conflict: Skilled Labor Shortage and Ethical Controversies

Human-machine collaboration will inevitably replace a large number of low-skilled workers. Without comprehensive retraining and reskilling programs, this could widen the employment market gap. Furthermore, "controlled machine collaboration," where robots transition from executors to decision supporters, raises ethical questions about the limits of machine power and responsibility.

Conclusion and Outlook

Human-machine collaboration is driving the manufacturing industry into a new era characterized by efficiency, flexibility, and intelligence. This technological paradigm not only optimizes production models but also redefines the role of humans and the boundaries of technical collaboration. Although challenges currently exist in the areas of cost, qualification, and ethics, with a sustainable development approach and collective effort, human-machine collaboration can become an indispensable driving force for reshaping the global economy in the coming decades.

Moreover, AI promotes the widespread application of human-machine collaboration in the manufacturing industry. Unlike traditional fixed automation devices, AI-supported collaborative robots can flexibly respond to a variety of production scenarios and perform complex tasks together with human workers. This approach to enhancing flexibility not only increases the speed of market adaptation but also strengthens the resilience of production systems against global supply chain challenges.

2.7 Real-Time Demand Forecasting and Inventory Management

As an integral part of modern corporate management, intelligent supply chain management has reached a new stage of development and demonstrated extraordinary transformation potential, thanks to the progress in the field of AI. Faced with the uncertainties and complexities of supply chains, the limitations of traditional management methods are becoming increasingly evident, while AI transforms the supply chain from a reactive approach to a proactive forecasting and control system through data modeling, advanced algorithms, and real-time analysis. This transformation not only enhances the efficiency and agility of the supply chain but also redefines the competitive strategies and business models of companies in dynamic markets. In the field of demand forecasting and inventory optimization, AI enables precise insights into market trends and consumer behavior through multilayered data analysis. This allows companies to plan inventory based on demand, increase turnover rates, and avoid unnecessary stockpiles. By predicting fluctuations in supply and demand, companies can dynamically adjust production and distribution plans to quickly respond to changes in external circumstances – this advantage is particularly significant in seasonal or event-driven industries. However, the importance of data quality and coverage becomes apparent in this process. As companies often face data silos and cannot guarantee the completeness and consistency of data, this poses a central challenge for the effective implementation of AI. In the logistics and transportation phase, AI-driven route planning and dynamic dispatch optimize resource utilization. By integrating real-time traffic data, transportation costs, and warehouse distribution, AI can create optimal delivery plans, thereby reducing delivery times and lowering operating costs. At the same time, the high responsiveness of AI makes supply chains more resilient in the face of unexpected events, a key advantage for globally operating multinational companies. However, without adequate infrastructure such as sensor networks or cloud computing resources, it may be difficult to utilize the highly complex AI systems for real-time tasks. Supply chain risk management is another example of the comprehensive empowerment by AI technologies. By monitoring supplier information, political changes, and natural disasters, AI models can predict potential risks and suggest mitigation measures. This capability reduces the vulnerability of companies to external disruptions and enhances the stability of the entire supply chain. However, building an effective risk management system depends not only on the collection of historical data but also requires the openness and standardization of data flows across different platforms. However, the fragmented ecosystems between industries greatly hinder the necessary cooperation. In addition to technological challenges, the comprehensive implementation of AI in supply chain management is also influenced by corporate culture and management models. The uncertainties regarding the high investment costs of AI systems and their returns pose the traditional management level with the task of finding a balance between technology investment and short-term returns. Moreover, as the integration of AI into the supply chain increases, concerns about data privacy and ethics are also growing, including the sensitivity of data, biases of algorithms, and transparency of decisions. These issues not only involve the social acceptance of technology but also the brand image and public trust in companies. The transition from linear chains to complex networks is the ultimate goal of AI-supported supply chain development. By creating comprehensive data sharing and cooperation between all supply chain links, companies can overcome organizational boundaries and achieve systemic efficiency gains and win-win opportunities. Despite the many obstacles in the process of technological implementation, the AI-supported intelligent supply chain will undoubtedly become the central driving force for competitive advantage in the future business world, provided that sound decisions are made and orderly progress is achieved.

From Data to Decisions

Faced with an increasingly complex market environment, companies are gradually shifting their supply chain management from traditional experience-based approaches to data-driven models. In this process, optimizing inventory structure based on accurate forecasting poses a central challenge to enhancing resource utilization efficiency and competitiveness. AI, with its deep learning and high-performance computing capabilities, can break through the limitations of traditional methods and elevate demand forecasting and inventory management to a new level that is real-time, dynamic, and intelligent. This section explores how AI enables the complete optimization chain from data analysis to decision support and examines its practical implementation and challenges in complex supply chain settings.

Market and Data in Harmony: Redefining Demand Forecasting

How AI Increases Forecasting Accuracy

Traditional demand planning is often limited by data scarcity, inadequate consideration of variable relationships, and lagging model forecasts. These approaches often fail to cope with dynamic market changes and sporadic disruptions. AI brings about a revolutionary change through the combination of various algorithms and dynamic data modeling:

Analysis of Multidimensional Data Relationships: AI can integrate and analyze sales trends, consumer trends, industry information, weather data, and sentiment analysis from various sources to create a comprehensive forecasting perspective.

Self-Adaptability: Dynamic models based on deep learning have the ability to optimize themselves autonomously, correct forecasting deviations in real time, and adapt to changing market conditions.

Anomaly Detection: AI uses time series analysis and forecasting deviation assessment methods to quickly identify external disruptive factors, such as sudden events, holiday peaks, or regional demand fluctuations, thereby avoiding erroneous decisions.

Case: Intelligent Forecasting in the Consumer Goods Industry

A global food company introduced an AI-supported demand forecasting platform to reshape its market response mechanisms. The platform analyzed historical consumer purchase data, seasonal influences, and online search trends to capture consumer dynamics. During a spontaneous market campaign, the AI system timely recommended replenishing stocks of high-demand products and offered a mobile restocking option for inefficient distribution points. Within a short period, inventory accuracy was increased by 20%, and logistics costs were reduced by 12%.

AI and Inventory Optimization: From Reacting to Proactive Management

Intelligent algorithms are revolutionizing inventory management. Inventory management is the cornerstone of supply chain efficiency. AI enables a profound transformation of traditional strategies through data-driven learning and automated decision-making. Particularly noteworthy characteristics include:

Dynamic Tiering: With AI-supported classification algorithms, inventories can be segmented into priority levels based on sales frequency, profitability, and market volatility, and controlled flexibly (e.g., dynamic ABC analysis).

Automated Reordering Strategies: AI combines inventory replenishment models with optimization algorithms to dynamically shape ideal reorder quantities and cycles, thereby reducing waste at the source.

Demand Detection and Agile Response: AI systems can predict potential imbalances between supply and demand and initiate immediate response plans to maintain business continuity during demand peaks or supply chain disruptions.

Case: Inventory Planning in the Industrial Supply Chain

A manufacturer of industrial equipment, which operates a global production and spare parts supply network, had difficulties with inventory overhangs and a lack of coordination of cross-border logistics processes. By using AI optimization tools, the company was able to integrate logistics data and inventory reports in real time, leading to the development of more flexible and regionally coordinated inventory strategies. The result: An improvement of over 25% in the turnover rate for core spare parts and a reduction of total supply chain costs by 16%.

Real-Time Technologies and Collaborative Analytics: Building a New Engine for Intelligent Supply Chains

Overturning Traditional Monitoring and Response Mechanisms in the Supply Chain

The complexity of supply chain operations requires efficiently coordinated approaches. AI addresses the core problems of information dispersion and long response times through multilayered technological innovations:

Real-Time Integration of the IoT: Intelligent sensors installed at all points of the supply chain transmit real-time inventory status, transportation information, and operational environment data to provide AI with precise inputs.
Dynamic Feedback Loop Optimization: AI combines flow modeling with digital twins of supply chains, simulates dynamic operational scenarios, and offers the best adaptation paths and parameters in real time.
Promoting Cross-Departmental Collaboration: AI-based supply chain data platforms connect internal departments with external partners, eliminate information barriers, and enhance decision-making and response consistency.
Case: Intelligent Monitoring in Cold Chain Logistics

An international refrigerated transport company has implemented AI and digital twins to monitor the entire logistics process in real time. When weather-related traffic disruptions occurred in a region, the AI system predicted potential delay risks and promptly adjusted transportation routes. The affected goods were immediately redirected to the optimal paths, ensuring that perishable food reached its destination in time and avoiding significant transportation losses.

Technological Challenges and Future Prospects: Accelerating Breakthroughs and Developments

Current Bottlenecks: The Problem of "Dual Coordination" Between Technology and Management

Despite the impressive efficiency gains in demand management and inventory optimization through AI, several hurdles remain:
Heterogeneity of Data Distribution: Differences in data capture and availability at various nodes make it difficult for AI models to achieve a global perspective.
Implementation Challenges: Some industries have high adaptability requirements for AI solutions, making existing universal models not directly transferable.
Ethical and Security Concerns: The increasing amount of sensitive business data used for AI training raises questions of data privacy and regulatory compliance. Balancing optimization and security remains an ongoing challenge.

Promoting Symbiosis Between Technology and Application

This symbiosis is enabled through dynamic cooperation models. The introduction of blockchain-based mechanisms for trustworthy data exchange across multiple nodes can enhance transparency of supply and demand in all phases. The balance between environment and economy can be achieved through the development of more energy-efficient AI algorithms. This can reduce the CO_2 footprint generated by model calculations and support sustainable supply chain development. Finally, transparent and interactive decision-making is also enabled. The development of AI-supported tools with highly interpretable interfaces is important to help users understand complex forecasts and promote acceptance of these results.

Conclusion and Insights

Real-time demand forecasting and inventory management form the core areas of intelligent supply chains. The integration of AI opens up new possibilities: from enhancing forecasting accuracy, optimizing inventory strategies to the real-time responsiveness of systems. AI fundamentally transforms traditional operational models, offering companies not only strategic advantages but also strengthening their ability to cope with market fluctuations. However, overcoming real challenges and fully exploiting potential opportunities require in-depth coordination between technology and management. In the future, with the continuous progress of intelligent technologies, AI-optimized supply chains may play a key role in promoting global trade resilience and sustainable resource utilization.

2.8 Transportation and Logistics: The Reality and Future of AI

With the deepening of the global economy and the rapid changes in consumer demand, the transportation and logistics industry is undergoing a profound structural transformation. Traditional logistics models are increasingly showing weaknesses in adapting to complex supply chains and volatile market demands. The comprehensive application of AI in this sector offers unparalleled optimization potential, from route planning and dynamic dispatch to enhancing customer experience, and drives the logistics system toward precision, efficiency, and sustainability.

The Core Competence of AI: Empowering the Entire Logistics Chain

The core of AI lies in its ability to process complex data and make intelligent decisions. This capability supports the optimization of the entire logistics chain and permeates all aspects from procurement, warehousing, transportation to delivery.

The Evolution of Intelligent Route Planning

As the foundation of logistics traffic, route planning directly affects transportation efficiency, costs, and environmental impact. Compared to static rules or linear algorithms, AI-supported route planning offers dynamic perception and real-time decision-making capabilities:

Integration of Multidimensional Real-Time Data: AI can combine traffic congestion, weather changes, construction information, and real-time vehicle positions to create vehicle-specific optimal routes. For example, an AI-supported transportation management system can avoid traffic-heavy roads during peak hours, thereby reducing both delivery time and fuel consumption simultaneously.
Agile Optimization Through Algorithmic Integration: Utilizing generic algorithms, reinforcement learning, and other intelligent techniques, optimization is achieved in complex transportation environments. For example, logistics giant FedEx has significantly improved the efficiency of its global logistics network through AI algorithms that take into account time windows, weight limits, and cost constraints.
Targeted Development of Emergency Scenarios: In cases of unpredictable events such as earthquakes or floods, AI can adjust route planning in real time and develop safe and efficient emergency delivery plans. This agility greatly reduces the risk of supply chain disruptions and enhances the industry's resilience.

Precision Through Dynamic Dispatch Technology

Faced with rising transportation costs and increasing delivery demands, optimizing resource utilization has become crucial. AI has made outstanding innovations in dynamic dispatch and resource configuration:

Intelligent Order Allocation and Loading Optimization: AI algorithms analyze the classification of orders by volume and weight to enable optimal packaging and vehicle loading. For example, DHL's intelligent distribution system avoids empty and overloaded vehicles, increasing resource utilization per transportation task by 15%.
Integration of Warehouse and Transportation Networks: Through the application of AI, warehousing and distribution systems are interconnected, allowing orders to be processed simultaneously based on real-time inventory data and route planning. This not only reduces delivery times but also optimizes warehouse turnover rates. JD Logistics' platform, which offers second-level sorting and minute-level response, has created an advantage in the instant delivery market.
Incorporation of Autonomous Delivery Systems: In distribution centers and urban logistics hubs, AI-supported autonomous vehicles and warehouse robots can implement efficient automatic sorting and delivery of goods, thereby reducing the time and costs of downstream logistics processes.

Precise Delivery and Transformation of Customer Experience

Logistics services are increasingly moving toward a "customer-oriented" approach, where AI enables companies to achieve higher customer satisfaction at lower cost structures.

Visualized Interaction Systems

Using location data and AI analytics engines, logistics companies can offer customers real-time updates on delivery routes, estimated arrival times, and support for last-minute changes, significantly enhancing the customer experience. This is primarily achieved through the following technologies:

Differentiated Delivery Networks for Sensitive Regions: AI models combine geographic heatmaps and consumer data to tailor so-called "last-mile" solutions. By utilizing micro-warehousing nodes, deliveries can be made directly, efficiently, and personalized.

Voice and Text Interaction Systems: Through AI-driven NLP, customer inquiries can be precisely recognized and answered more quickly, with more complex cases being escalated to human dispatchers. Amazon's Alexa Logistics Assistant is an example of such an ecosystem for intelligent customer service.

Sustainability Innovations in Environmental and Cost Perspectives

Efficient transport optimization is not only a key aspect of business success but also plays a vital role in the transition to a sustainable economy.

Promoting Emission-Free and Sustainable Transport

The high fuel consumption of the traditional logistics industry has led to significant CO_2 emissions. AI helps achieve these goals through various control approaches:

Route Optimization to Prevent Fuel Waste

Route optimizations that prevent fuel waste directly contribute to reducing the carbon footprint. For example, UPS achieved annual savings of thousands of liters of fuel and a reduction of 30,000 tons of CO_2 emissions through its ORION project. In parallel, AI is used for the dispatch of electric vehicle fleets and their strategic charging stations, supporting efforts for a sustainable electric vehicle transportation infrastructure.

Cost Reduction and Flexible Supply Chains

From a business perspective, AI-based intelligent logistics solutions bring significant improvements to the economic structures of companies:

Inventory and Transport Link Optimizations

Warehouse and transport link optimizations, as well as inventory optimizations, enable cost reductions of 20–35%. At the same time, better processing of order entries increases profits. AI technology also allows for flexible adaptation of the supply chain during crises, thereby reducing inventory losses, securing inventory capital, and comprehensively strengthening organizational resilience.

Technological Challenges and the Balance of Value Creation

The penetration of the logistics industry with AI also brings profound challenges that require industry-wide solutions:

Regulation of Data Security

The logistics industry is characterized by high data volumes, including consumer behavior, business activities, and collaboration data. Orderly handling of data privacy and information security is crucial for the sustainable introduction of AI.

Technological Costs and Imbalance of Corporate Resources

The high costs of AI implementation put significant financial pressure on smaller companies. Differences in technological infrastructure or human capital further exacerbate market inequality.

Societal Conflicts Between Employment and Technology

Although AI significantly increases efficiency, there is already a shift in the employment structure, which could lead to social tensions in the medium term. Both companies and state and societal institutions are called upon to develop appropriate measures and support mechanisms.

The Future of Automation and Autonomous Systems

With the rapid development of AI and related technologies, the era of "fully automated logistics" is approaching. Particularly noteworthy are:

Autonomous Long-Haul Logistics

Companies like Waymo and Tesla are already conducting pilot projects for autonomous trucks and drones in several US states, which could revolutionize global long-haul logistics.

Unmanned Drone Deliveries

Through the combination of 5G and AI technologies, drone logistics solutions such as medical emergency supply or coverage of remote areas could quickly become a reality.

Decentralized Cooperation via Blockchain

With AI algorithms and secure blockchain infrastructures, self-organized logistics networks could be made more transparent, efficient, and traceable.

Conclusion: A Logistics Roadmap for the Intelligent Age

The transformation of transport and logistics driven by AI is not only a matter of efficiency but also a cornerstone of modern economic systems. Long-term influence, however, requires the integration of technology, economic visions, as well as social and political cooperation, to create a sustainable and equitable ecosystem for the logistics of the future.

2.9 Risk Management: The Shield of the Intelligent Supply Chain

The global supply chain is evolving toward complexity and diversification, while simultaneously revealing its vulnerable aspects. Geopolitical conflicts, natural disasters, and pandemics are occurring with increasing frequency, posing significant challenges to the stability of the supply chain. Traditional risk management models often react very slowly, are based solely on empirical values, and lack the flexibility to respond to sudden changes.

Meeting the Challenges of the Age of Uncertainty

Against this backdrop of disruption, AI is developing into a powerful tool for managing risks in the supply chain, from prediction to real-time intervention. It has the potential to fundamentally transform risk management.

AI does not replace human decision-making. Instead, it provides insights and recommendations that help companies respond more efficiently to complex situations. The focus of supply chain risk management has shifted from reactive problem-solving to proactive prediction and real-time adaptation. Companies are not only using technology for "crisis management" but are increasingly focusing on "stability optimization" and "resilience."

The Key Role of AI in Supply Chain Risk Management

Data-Driven Risk Detection and Early Warning

The primary task of supply chain risk management is the precise identification of potential problems in order to take measures at an early stage. With advanced technologies such as ML and data processing, AI comprehensively analyzes heterogeneous data from the supply chain. It not only identifies obvious risks but also detects hidden dangers. Application examples include:

Integration of IoT Data: AI analyzes data from sensors and real-time monitoring devices such as transportation routes, warehouse capacities, and port traffic. By learning from historical patterns, it can detect unusual activities and risks early on, such as route congestion, delivery delays, or excess inventory levels.

Analysis of Political and Geopolitical Dynamics: With the help of NLP, AI can extract relevant events from news, government announcements, and social media, such as export restrictions or fluctuations in trade policies, which serve as decision-making aids.

Data-driven risk detection enhances visualization and real-time analysis, providing managers with a more comprehensive information base. In particular, in scenarios with overwhelmingly large amounts of data, automated analysis by AI offers significant relief.

Dynamic Scenario Simulation and Forecasting Capabilities

Another central contribution of AI lies in the modeling and forecasting of potential risk scenarios. With the following capabilities, companies can make well-founded decisions:

Simulation of Demand Fluctuations: Based on sales data and macroeconomic trends, AI forecasts changes in supply and demand. This helps companies adjust their production and inventory plans to avoid supply disruptions due to market saturation or sudden spikes in demand.

Scenarios for Catastrophe Impact: Using available geographical and meteorological data, AI simulates the potential impact of natural disasters such as storms or earthquakes on critical supply chain processes. Companies can optimize logistics routes and also adjust optional inventory and storage.

Supplier Risk Assessment: AI aggregates historical data from suppliers (e.g., punctuality of deliveries or contract breaches) and creates forecasts for potential problems. It also suggests alternative suppliers to minimize dependency and concentration risks.

This proactive forecasting capability extends risk management beyond merely reacting to existing crises by uncovering potential future problems. Companies thus gain higher planning certainty in an increasingly complex global environment.

Real-Time Intervention and Resilience Optimization

Relying solely on warnings and forecasts to deal with sudden events is not sufficient. The ability to implement immediate solutions supported by AI is a crucial competitive advantage in supply chain management. AI offers rapid response options, minimizes the impact of risks, and limits potential damage. Examples include:

Automatic Adjustment of Logistics Network: If AI detects a delay or uncontrollable factor at a logistics point, it immediately adjusts the distribution of goods, for example by rerouting orders to backup warehouses or activating a multipoint delivery strategy.

Prioritization of Transportation Decisions: When there are disruptions in several transportation chains, AI models can prioritize transportation resources based on urgency, order value, and customer requirements to maintain core business activities.

Real-Time Evaluation of Alternatives: AI calculates the pros and cons of different scenarios in real time, for example by comparing the costs of alternative supplier contracts or analyzing the transportation costs of alternative routes, and provides visually prepared suggestions for decision-making support.

This not only significantly reduces the complexity of decision-making for managers but also greatly increases the precision and efficiency of countermeasures.

Case Examples: AI Enables Complex Risk Management

Global Medical Supply Chain: Dealing with Multiple Risks

During the COVID-19 pandemic, the supply chain of an international manufacturer of medical devices was thrown into crisis due to global logistical restrictions. The company integrated the AI-supported tools depicted below to consolidate supply chain data in real time:

The AI analyzed logistics stress data of regional transport services and dynamically re-evaluated customer-related orders with a high probability of delay.

For particularly risky regions or countries, the AI recommended activating additional suppliers and incorporating flexible clauses into supply contracts (e.g., accepting delivery delays).

Forecast models optimized the best route for transporting the devices used in vaccine production, taking into account weather conditions and cross-border customs factors.

Through such a multifunctional risk minimization strategy, the company ensured the global availability of emergency materials, reduced bottlenecks in order management during critical periods, and kept costs below the industry average.

Intelligent Retail: Resilience Management

A large retail company implemented an AI-based intelligent control tool for its distribution network, which demonstrated impressive resilience during peak times such as sales holidays. The potential delays predicted by AI were caused by staff shortages at regular transport hubs. The AI organized autonomous delivery solutions in advance to accelerate loading and unloading processes. Through ML models, the AI optimized regional replenishment quantities in real time, prioritizing popular products and better handling demand spikes.

This approach not only maximized the operational efficiency of retail logistics but also minimized the risk of delivery failures during highly volatile periods.

Technological Breakthroughs and Future Prospects

1. Integration of Large-Scale Risk Models
   Future advancements in AI-driven risk management will depend on the development of large-scale integration models that combine weather, energy market, traffic, and political dynamics to create detailed risk analysis matrices for companies. This will significantly enhance the ability for multidimensional risk monitoring.
2. The Rise of XAI
   The transparency of AI-proposed decisions is a central key to the acceptance of future technologies. With XAI, companies can understand the logical framework behind AI decisions, place more trust in them, and make well-founded strategic adjustments.
3. Trustworthy Data and Blockchain Interaction

The use of blockchain for validating real-time data will fundamentally transform supply chain data management. It will prevent inaccurate risk assessments due to fake data or lost historical information. Trustworthy data will form the basis for improving the accuracy of AI predictions.

Balancing Ethics and Technological Risks

However, the rapid development of AI also poses ethical and technical challenges that need to be addressed:

Algorithm Transparency: It must be ensured that AI systems are not based on biases or inferior data sets, as this could lead to wrong decisions in risk management.

Environmental Fairness: Small suppliers could be excluded from an AI ecosystem due to a lack of technical resources. Integrated technological solutions are needed to overcome such barriers.

Responsibility in Regulation: Clear legal frameworks must be created to regulate risks associated with failed AI-supported interventions and resulting disputes.

These challenges show that technological progress must be accompanied by supportive social policy measures to ensure fairness and justice.

Conclusion

AI not only improves the operational speed of supply chains but also influences the strategic planning of risk management. It gives companies more resilience and proactivity by transforming complex management tasks into efficient, intelligent solutions. As technology continues to evolve, AI will become indispensable for future management systems. However, real transformation does not only take place in increasing efficiency but in the shared responsibility to create a more stable and just global supply chain structure.

2.10 Digital Marketing and Personalized Recommendation Systems

AI offers entirely new strategic perspectives and technological capabilities for digital marketing and the acquisition of customer insights. Its potential for precise analysis of user needs and optimization of marketing strategies is undeniable. Through deep learning algorithms, AI can extract valuable, previously hidden commercial information from vast amounts of data. Companies can not only capture market dynamics in real time but also reliably predict user behavior to make data-driven strategic decisions. In a highly competitive environment, this market transparency becomes a crucial tool for securing market share and success.

A central application example is the personalized recommendation system, which is based on the analysis of user data and behavioral patterns. Whether it is about recommending products on e-commerce platforms or content on streaming services: this technology optimizes the user experience through highly precise content matching, strengthens brand loyalty, and significantly increases conversion rates. Its value is not only reflected in short-term gains or increased traffic but also in establishing long-term customer relationships for companies. In addition, the in-depth analysis of big data by AI enables dynamic optimization in resource allocation, market segmentation, and the development of core strategies. This supports the transformation from traditional experience-based to data-driven marketing logic.

Advances in AI in the field of emotion recognition also have significant impacts. Advanced NLP technologies enable AI to detect emotions and needs of users from social media and online reviews. Companies can use these insights to evaluate their brand perception and take corresponding measures, whether through adjustments of advertising content, crisis communication strategies, or product designs. For example, real-time monitoring of negative emotions can help companies quickly respond to potential brand crises and minimize damage. This emotional interaction is central to personalized user experiences, promoting brand loyalty, and preventing reputation risks.

Automation tools further advance the practical application of AI in managing the customer journey. These tools integrate predictive and optimization models, enabling companies to track the entire user path, communicate personally, and conduct performance measurements. The data-driven management philosophy not only increases the flexibility and precision of marketing initiatives but also supports the development of systematic strategies for the entire customer life cycle. However, the implementation of such technologies also poses challenges: on the one hand, large amounts of high-quality training data are needed; on the other hand, global data protection and data ethics regulations must be considered. Balancing maximum data utilization with social responsibility will become a central issue for companies.

Another risk lies in the potential over-reliance on AI in marketing. The ability to respond precisely to complex situations cannot fully replace a strategic and holistic perspective. If executives rely solely on AI model results and neglect other important variables, it can lead to strategic misdecisions. Companies must go beyond mere technological dependence and seamlessly integrate AI into the strategic thinking of management to ensure the best possible collaboration between technology and corporate leadership. AI is not only a key driver of global corporate strategies but also a mirror to reflect on the ethics of business logic and technological boundaries. Its application path must always be guided by the principles of fairness, sustainability, and the protection of user rights in order to achieve business goals while also taking on social responsibility.

Personalized Recommendation Systems

The Bridge to Capturing User Needs

In the age of information overload, users expect quick solutions that meet their needs, while companies aim to reach users effectively and boost transactions. Personalized recommendation systems are the technological tool that brings these expectations and goals together. By leveraging AI and big data analytics, they enable precise matching of users with products, content, and services, thereby optimizing user experience and business success. This technology has already penetrated areas such as e-commerce, streaming services, education, and news, becoming a growth engine for the global information economy.

Precise Detection of User Preferences

The core of personalized recommendation systems lies in the collection and analysis of user behavior data to predict future interests and needs. Using advanced algorithms, these systems generate individualized recommendations and provide efficient distribution of products and services. Here are some of the main methods used in practical applications:

Collaborative Filtering: This analyzes the similarity of user behavior or product usage patterns to identify "collaborative commonalities." Based on the principle of "birds of a feather flock together," the system builds a recommendation system based on user interests. For example, if a user purchases product A, the system recommends other products that are often bought together with A. This method is widely used on e-commerce websites but can be limited by computational power when dealing with large amounts of data.

Content-Based Recommendations: This approach analyzes the attribute tags of products or services and compares them with user preferences. Whether it is online courses, playlists, or recommended movies on streaming platforms, the precision of this method is crucial. For example, a video platform can derive preferences from movie plots, director styles, or actors and recommend films that may interest the user.

Hybrid Recommendation Models: Since individual algorithms are limited by data dimensions, hybrid models combine collaborative filtering and content-based approaches. By applying dynamic weighting, personalized recommendations are significantly improved, especially in scenarios involving mixed interests and categories.

Technologies and Strategies to Increase Conversion Rates

Personalized recommendation systems not only optimize the presentation of information and products but also activate user needs, increasing conversion rates and customer loyalty. The following technologies offer specific solutions for the successful implementation of recommendation systems:

Real-Time Calculation and Dynamic Adjustments: Real-time recommendations represent the cutting edge of recommendation systems. They create dynamic feedback based on users' current actions. For example, if a user conducts a product search on an e-commerce site, the system can derive their purchase intentions through "behavioral funnel analysis" and recommend relevant products or accessories in real time. These dynamic decision-making models open up new business opportunities, such as "recommended deals nearby" on online-to-offline (O2O) platforms.

Post Hoc Attribution Analysis: Improving recommendation strategies involves analyzing user data and continuous optimization. Click-through rates, purchasing behavior, and dwell time provide important information for algorithm adjustments. For example, an online fashion platform can analyze evaluations and return patterns after product recommendations to develop smarter recommendation models for repeat purchases.

Multichannel Recommendation Management: Effective recommendation systems cover both online and offline channels to ensure a consistent user experience. For example, based on a product a user has searched for on the mobile phone, companies can offer instant discounts in their physical stores to promote integrated purchasing decisions. This strategy greatly increases efficiency and user-friendliness.

Applications for Personalization

The cases for personalized recommendation systems are diverse and adaptable to the requirements of different industries. The key lies in embedding algorithm capabilities into specific business models to maximize value:

E-commerce: Precise Promotion and Dynamic Shelf Optimization

Amazon is a classic example of the application of recommendation algorithms. Through large-scale data analysis, its system predicts the consumption preferences of each individual user by integrating various recommendation processes (such as "combo offers" or "comparisons of similar items") into the shopping experience. This strategy not only increases users' willingness to purchase but also improves the platform's inventory turnover.

Media: Frequent Content Distribution and Higher User Engagement

Netflix optimizes personalized content display through its recommendation system, ensuring that each user receives a unique homepage with relevant suggestions. The system considers not only preferences for specific movie categories but also usage intentions (e.g., entertainment, learning, or leisure), thereby significantly enhancing loyalty and subscription renewal rates.

Education: Adaptive Learning Models

Educational recommendation systems not only facilitate efficient knowledge transfer but also tailor learning paths through adaptive models. For example, an online education platform dynamically recommends an individual learning plan based on error analysis, learning speed, and course preferences. Users do not need to manually filter courses, as the system automatically provides optimal learning resources, enabling "unique learning paths."

Technological Challenges and Practical Issues

Despite the widespread application of recommendation systems, more and more technical limitations and practical challenges are emerging:

Data Privacy and Compliance

Recommendation systems rely heavily on user behavioral data, which often poses the risk of personal data misuse. In light of increasingly stringent data protection regulations (such as the GDPR, General Data Protection Regulation of the EU), the secure and transparent use of data is a global challenge. Solutions include the adoption of technologies like federated learning, which minimizes the risk of data loss and empowers users with control over their data.

Recommendation Fatigue and Algorithmic Limits

Boring or overly frequent recommendations can fatigue users and lead to rejection. The solution lies in increasing the dynamism of user profiles, considering various dimensions of their needs, and avoiding overfitting with bias-free algorithms.

Cold Start and Long-Tail Processing

Recommendations often fall short of expectations for new users and less popular content. This is the traditional "cold start" problem, where new users do not have satisfactory experiences, and less popular products are inadequately considered. Promising approaches to solving this problem include the use of generative adversarial networks, which enable recommendations in data-sparse contexts.

Inspirational Considerations and Future Perspectives

The development of personalized recommendation systems is just the beginning of intelligent business models. Future technology will continue to evolve in the following directions:

Integration of Multimodal Data

Beyond analyzing text or user behavior, the next generation of recommendation systems will incorporate more complex data such as images, language, and biometric signals. For example, systems could recommend furniture that matches the style of uploaded room images.

Context-Based and "Invisible" Recommendations

The future of recommendations will shift further from clear push notifications to subtle, context-aware suggestions. AR technologies in smart devices or household items could integrate recommendation systems and offer user-friendly services "exactly where they are needed."

Community-Oriented Optimization Algorithms

Personalized recommendation services will evolve from individual optimization to community orientation. By analyzing community behavior patterns in social networks, systems can promote synchronized consumption actions within specific interest groups and enhance the effects of sharing and linking.

Conclusion

The core task of personalized recommendation systems is not only to redefine individual service but also to serve as a blueprint for data-driven business models. With further technological development and regulation, recommendation systems will become smarter, more differentiated, and more explainable while preserving privacy. Companies must not only build technical capabilities but also maintain the balance between business and social responsibilities to create a sustainable foundation for an intelligent living environment.

2.11 Marketing Data Analysis

Data is increasingly becoming a core competency in modern marketing. It serves not only to explain market phenomena but also to uncover behavioral patterns and potential opportunities. With the groundbreaking developments in AI, companies can gain deeper insights from vast amounts of marketing data to optimize business decisions and strategic planning. Through AI-driven analysis tools, marketing teams can systematically solve complex data problems and elevate resource efficiency and user experience to new levels.

This section focuses on AI-powered marketing data analysis. Using specific application examples and technological frameworks, it explores how AI can break through the boundaries of traditional marketing, redefine decision-making logic, and analyze the central challenges and solutions in the introduction of technology.

Challenges and Solutions in Cross-Platform Marketing

In the context of digital transformation, the marketing environment has become increasingly complex, and cross-platform working has become the norm. From social media to search engines, and from content marketing to e-commerce platforms, data sources are more diverse than ever. These fragmented characteristics pose significant challenges to companies in terms of resource allocation and campaign optimization.

AI offers companies new methods to tackle these challenges in cross-platform marketing. Through deep learning and big data models, AI is capable of integrating heterogeneous data from various platforms to deliver comprehensive behavioral maps and decision recommendations. The advantage of AI lies not only in precise analysis but also in real-time adaptation and optimization, enabling companies to actively respond to environmental changes and transform data insights into actionable measures.

Example: Intelligent Marketing Optimization of a Global Retail Company

In this example, a global retail company faced the challenge of inefficient resource allocation in Facebook, Instagram, and Google ad campaigns. By introducing an AI-driven data analysis platform, the company achieved the following improvements:

On Instagram, it was found that video ads achieved significantly higher conversion rates among the target group of women aged 25–34 compared to other formats.

Google Ads were used to attract more first-time buyers, while Facebook Ads had a stronger user retention function.

Based on these insights, the company adjusted its budget, focusing 70% of resources on the most effective channels and optimizing content. These strategies led to an increase in campaign ROI by more than 25% and a significant improvement in customer loyalty.

Data Integration and Dynamic Collaboration Systems

Optimizing marketing initiatives requires data integration. With the help of AI, information silos can be broken down, and fragmented data from various platforms can be consolidated into a single structure. In this area, AI offers two unique advantages:

- Unified Data Transformation: Using intelligent data preprocessing tools, AI can standardize data from different platforms while avoiding duplication or loss.
- Dynamic Multifactor Recognition: AI conducts in-depth analysis of the data parameters of each campaign and quantifies their contribution to effectiveness, such as the dynamic correlation between click-through rate and conversion rate.

Technological Framework: Collaborative Marketing Based on Generative AI

The use of generative AI makes data integration and campaign coordination even more agile. This process is not limited to content generation but also includes real-time adaptation of strategies and their intelligent processing. For example, a marketing team can generate behavioral forecasts based on an AI platform and dynamically adjust ad placements according to the current click status. Once specific user groups receive personalized content, their interaction rate significantly increases.

Individual Optimization of Resource Allocation

Traditional models of resource allocation often rely on fixed rules or statistical analyses. However, AI can enable more precise and dynamic resource allocation through reinforcement learning and deep learning. AI conducts real-time analyses and creates predictive models to provide personalized recommendations for resource deployment and budget planning. This capability significantly enhances resource efficiency, allowing companies not only to save costs but also to strengthen user engagement through targeted actions.

The Introduction Mechanism of AI into Resource Allocation

In scenario simulation, AI models data using supervised learning and dynamically adjusts resource allocation strategies based on expected outcomes and predictive analytics. This is followed by dynamic feedback optimization. After each campaign, the AI tool iteratively updates the strategies based on the results and redirects the budget toward the most effective measures.

Example: Resource Optimization of an E-commerce Platform

An e-commerce platform utilized AI-supported resource optimization tools to analyze the interest profiles of different user groups and create personalized recommendation models. It was found that users with high purchase frequency responded strongly to time-limited offers, while users with low activity were more interested in long-term discounts. Based on the AI model's recommendations, the company reallocated its resources accordingly, which increased both the campaign conversion rate and purchase frequency.

User Behavior Prediction and Adaptive Strategies

Another significant benefit of AI in marketing analysis is the prediction of user behavior. By conducting in-depth analysis of usage data, AI can forecast future customer needs and thus align marketing campaigns more effectively. This not only minimizes the risk of customer churn but also maximizes the overall efficiency of the campaigns.

An AI-supported prediction system involves the following key process steps:

Dynamic Updating of User Profiles: Comprehensive analysis of user behavior trends and historical preferences to make predictions as realistic as possible.

Modeling of Behavior Trends: Developing a predictive model that identifies future areas of interest for users and supports long-term marketing strategies.

Personalized Content Presentation: Dynamically adjusting content based on predictions to enhance user interaction.

Example: Behavioral Forecasting of an Online Education Platform

An online education platform analyzed the learning behavior of its users using AI and found that certain user groups were more active during evening hours, while others preferred shorter video content. Based on these insights, the platform adjusted its course offerings and added evening activities. This not only increased participation rates but also led to a significant increase in course bookings.

Ethical Challenges and Technological Regulation

In the field of marketing data analysis, ethical considerations and privacy protection are crucial. The boundaries of data collection and usage must be clearly defined to avoid damaging a company's reputation or risking legal consequences. The following measures can help companies align the use of technology with ethical principles:

Transparency: Establish clear data usage policies and communicate them openly to build user trust.

Anonymization: Encrypt and anonymize sensitive user data in all analysis phases.

Compliance Checks: Introduce automated compliance tools to ensure data usage adheres to relevant regulations such as GDPR or CCPA (California Consumer Privacy Act).

Industry Approach: Privacy-Oriented Optimization of Data Analysis

A fintech company developed a privacy-friendly AI analysis platform that encrypts user data throughout the process and implements dynamic access rights. This not only reduced ethical risks but also increased marketing efficiency. This approach also set new standards for data usage policies across the industry.

Summary and Development Trends

AI-driven marketing data analysis is evolving from a supportive tool to a strategic core element. Thanks to technological breakthroughs in cross-platform optimization, resource allocation, and behavior prediction, companies can generate measurable economic added value from data. At the same time, the widespread application of technologies places higher demands on topics such as data privacy and ethical regulation, which will influence future dissemination and acceptance.

With the further development of multimodal data, digital twins, and emotion recognition technologies, the field of marketing analysis will experience additional innovations. Companies must not only unlock the technical potential but also continue to explore the balance between consumer experience and resource efficiency in practice to open up new strategic possibilities.

Through in-depth data analysis and resource-efficient decision-making, marketing strategies will not only become more forward-looking but also deliver long-term social and economic benefits for companies.

2.12 Retail and E-Commerce

In the retail and e-commerce sectors, intelligent assistants are revolutionizing the interactions between businesses and customers. During search processes, they analyze purchase histories and predict customer needs to generate precise product recommendations. Companies like Amazon offer virtual shopping assistants that enable consumers to complete the entire shopping process, from product search to payment, through a chat interface, significantly simplifying the shopping experience.

The benefits of intelligent assistants in after sales service are also hard to overlook. They provide quick answers to questions or instructions on returns, allowing businesses to reduce the costs associated with traditional customer support teams. Combined with emotion recognition and multimodal interaction technology, the retail industry could become even more customer-specific in the future, further enhancing customer loyalty.

Assistants in the Industrial Internet of Things (IIoT)

In the industrial sector, intelligent assistants are massively increasing efficiency through real-time monitoring and coordination. For example, some manufacturing companies use digital assistants for machine inspections. These systems analyze production data, identify potential defects, and suggest repair measures to minimize unplanned downtime.

Another important application is as a virtual project manager responsible for planning tasks and dealing with risks. These assistants model production data, monitor key milestones, and provide real-time optimization suggestions, significantly improving team collaboration and project success rates. In industrial settings, intelligent assistants are increasingly becoming the "nervous system" for solving complex problems and driving the digital transformation of businesses.

Optimization of Efficiency and User Experience

The cross-industry application of intelligent assistants primarily demonstrates their potential for enhancing user experience and efficiency. These improvements involve the following areas:

- Simplifying tasks and saving time: Intelligent assistants automate repetitive tasks such as schedule management or document organization, allowing users to focus more on creative activities.
- Optimizing information and decision-making: By integrating big data and predictive models, assistants provide rational suggestions, such as expenditure forecasts in financial tools or optimal workout times in health applications.
- Designing more emotional interactions: With the help of multimodal technologies, assistants can recognize user emotions and adjust their communication accordingly, promoting more positive and enjoyable interactions.

These advancements not only meet the growing efficiency demands of users but also bring significant productivity gains to businesses.

Current Challenges and Future Development

Despite the widespread use of intelligent assistants, there are still numerous technical, ethical, and social challenges:

Data Privacy Risks: Since intelligent assistants collect and store a vast amount of personal data, the question arises of how to prevent misuse or data breaches. Transparent data management models and compliance with global data privacy regulations will continue to be essential.

Cultural and Linguistic Adaptability: The use of intelligent assistants in different cultural and linguistic contexts requires a high degree of technical adaptation. Complex language structures in certain regions or cultural differences can lead to misunderstandings or functional deficiencies. Therefore, the training of such systems needs to be more open and diverse.

Impact on the Labor Market: While intelligent assistants make many work areas more efficient, they are also gradually replacing human labor in certain professions. This poses social challenges regarding employment and requires a balance between technological progress and social responsibility.

Looking to the future, intelligent assistants could further evolve through emotional intelligence, cross-industry collaboration, and security mechanisms. With the help of quantum computing and artificial general intelligence, they could break through current functional limitations and develop into comprehensive digital partners that promote a harmonious coexistence between technology and humans.

Summary

The development and cross-industry application of intelligent assistants not only highlight the driving force of technological breakthroughs for productivity but also demonstrate the potential of human-machine collaboration to shape social changes. However, technological progress also requires ethical and responsible approaches. Data privacy, employment issues, and cultural adaptability will remain central themes for future development. In the future, intelligent assistants will be used more comprehensively and functionally advanced in daily life and industry, not only creating new value but also preparing society for a smarter and more sustainable future.

2.13 Social Media and Sentiment Analysis

In the age of digital information overload, social media serves not only as a vital platform for human interaction but also as a core area where companies can gain insights into user psychology, market dynamics, and competitive landscapes. AI-supported techniques for sentiment analysis have established themselves as effective tools for understanding user emotions and attitudes and have become indispensable for precise marketing, brand management, and crisis communication. However, challenges such as data bias, ethical risks, and context understanding still exist and urgently need to be addressed. This section will thoroughly investigate the technological approaches, innovative applications, and potential risks of sentiment analysis on social media and provide specific suggestions for future development.

Technology of Sentiment Analysis

Sentiment analysis leverages technologies such as NLP, Deep Learning, and multimodal approaches to extract emotional tendencies from unstructured data and generate understandable and actionable insights for businesses.

Natural Language Processing: Decoding the Language Structure of Emotion

The core of sentiment analysis lies in the semantic interpretation of text data. NLP technologies create a framework for emotion assessment through the following steps:

Emotional Lexicon Construction: Building a lexicon that includes important emotional expressions in natural language is a key task. For example, "good" and "bad" correspond to positive and negative emotions, respectively.

Syntactic Analysis: This involves the precise interpretation of ambiguities and sentence structures. For instance, "This product is of excellent quality, but the customer service is terrible" needs to separately analyze both positive and negative emotions.

Context-Aware Models: By analyzing the context of comments, these models can reduce misunderstandings. For example, "not bad" might indicate a positive emotion in a humorous context, while it could suggest criticism in a neutral comment.

Deep Learning: Enhancing the Accuracy of Emotion Detection

In recent years, deep learning has significantly enhanced the performance of sentiment analysis, especially with the remarkable progress made possible by pretrained language models such as BERT and GPT:

These models are capable of capturing complex emotional signals in language, such as metaphors, sarcasm, and subtle expressions. For example, the negative emotion in "the service is as disappointing as ever" can be successfully detected.

It also strengthens the ability to analyze multilingual content to better meet the needs of globally operating companies. Moreover, user behavior data can be comprehensively evaluated in conjunction with text semantics to identify emotional trends.

Multimodal Analysis: Capturing Non-verbal Emotions

For images, videos, and audio data, AI technologies enable emotion detection through multimodal approaches. For example, in live streaming, sentiment analysis can combine vocal intonations (changes in pitch or timbre) and facial expressions (micro-expression analysis) to assess the host's mood. This capability has already spread widely in areas such as live e-commerce, job evaluation, and mental health monitoring.

Breakthroughs and Application Scenarios for Companies

Sentiment analysis technologies are essential tools for companies to interpret user feedback, optimize services, and enhance competitiveness. The following examples illustrate typical application areas.

Case 1: Real-Time Brand Monitoring and Public Relations
Social media amplifies users' emotional reactions, and the speed of brand perception dissemination is unprecedented. Sentiment analysis tools provide companies with a real-time view of dynamic emotions, enabling them to quickly respond to potential reputation crises. A large retail company noticed an increasing number of user complaints about delivery delays on Twitter during "Black Friday." Sentiment analysis tools showed that the proportion of negative emotions quickly rose to 78%. As a crisis response, the company immediately adjusted its shipping announcements and strengthened its customer service team, thereby containing the spread of negative opinions on social media within 24 h.

Case 2: In-Depth Personalized Marketing Strategies
Sentiment analysis can not only understand users' brand perceptions but also create recommendations that better match users' emotional characteristics to improve user experience. For example, in dynamic marketing, AI may recommend high-end consumer goods to a user who has recently developed a positive mood, while showing soothing advertisements to a user with a negative mood. By analyzing user reactions to different advertising content, companies can target the highest-rated ads to optimize advertising effectiveness.

Case 3: Product Improvement Through User Feedback
Sentiment analysis provides companies with an objective means to identify problem areas and strengths of a product and continuously improve their product and service quality. A food company analyzed a large number of comments on social platforms and found that users are increasingly in favor of "low-sugar products" and expressed negative emotions about the high sugar content in the existing product range. The company quickly adjusted the recipes and launched new products. Feedback showed that the Net Promoter Score (NPS) increased by 30% afterward.

Case 4: Modeling the Emotional Spread During Crisis Events
Sentiment analysis technologies can predict the spread of negative emotions on social media during crisis communication, giving companies valuable time. For example, AI models can automatically create propagation path predictions in the early stages of an incident to help community management teams take targeted measures.

Challenges in Technological Implementation

Despite the significant commercial potential of sentiment analysis technologies, there are key challenges that companies must address. The three main challenges are outlined here:

Balancing Data Bias and Reliability

Due to the highly unstructured and diverse nature of social media data, models face the following challenges:

Data Bias: When the focus is too narrowly concentrated on a specific region or platform, data bias can occur, reducing the generalizability of the findings.

Processing Unconventional Expressions: When users employ emojis, slang, or combinations of punctuation to express emotions, existing algorithms often struggle to interpret these atypical data effectively.

Complexity of Emotional Context

Emotional expressions are context-dependent, and AI still tends to overlook contextual details. For example, the phrase "This is great" might express a positive sentiment, but in the context of "This lousy service is great," it conveys the opposite. Companies urgently need to implement advanced contextual modeling technologies to address this.

Data Privacy and Technological Ethics

Collecting data from social media for sentiment analysis quickly runs into privacy boundaries. Companies should strive to find a balance in the following areas:

- Clear Communication and Consent: It is essential to inform users clearly and obtain their consent before data collection.
- Anonymization of Results: To prevent excessive monitoring of user behavior, anonymizing analysis results is crucial.
- Compliance with Regulations: Adhering to data privacy laws and regulations (e.g., GDPR and CCPA) and establishing ethical practices in technology implementation are fundamental requirements.

Outlook and Conclusion

Sentiment analysis is rapidly evolving into the bridge between social media and commercial insights. With advancements in deep learning, multimodal technology, and semantic interpretation, this technology will create more value in areas such as advertising, brand management, marketing, and product improvement.

In the future, implementation will increasingly focus on holism and sustainability. For example, sentiment analysis could be combined with graph databases to represent connections between various data identities, such as users or content. Cross-border analysis of emotions across different languages and cultures will expand evaluations to include international application scenarios. However, companies must always consider the ethical risks associated with using such technologies and ensure that sentiment analyses are conducted in a fair and transparent framework.

Through the coordinated development of technology and regulation, sentiment analysis will not only continue to strengthen commercial practices but also contribute to the improvement of social communication and pave the way for a smarter, more empathetic digital ecosystem.

2.14 Supporting Entrepreneurship: AI as a New Path for Start-Ups

AI is revolutionizing the inner logic of entrepreneurship and innovation, evolving from a mere supportive tool to a central driver of profound changes in the start-up ecosystem. On a technical level, AI helps entrepreneurs decipher market complexity and quickly identify customer needs and trend dynamics through ML and data analysis. These precise insights provide a solid foundation for renewing and adapting business models, significantly reducing the costs of failures and missteps in start-ups, and optimizing resource allocation. Meanwhile, intelligent platforms based on big data and deep learning algorithms enable founders to access technology with lower barriers to entry, allowing them to focus more on their core strategic ideas and creative expressions. On an organizational level, AI is driving the development of innovation labs within companies. These efficient collaborative spaces facilitate a deep integration of technology and business. Through high-speed computing and model simulations, companies can redefine processes from idea generation to implementation. These labs use dynamic analysis tools to identify micro-changes in the technological environment, helping companies quickly adjust strategic decisions and create reliable pathways for entering new markets. This experimental and validation-driven agile concept enables companies to swiftly seize emerging business opportunities and transform them into multidimensional value creation. Additionally, AI is transforming knowledge management and collaboration models. AI-based intelligent platforms, relying on speech recognition and real-time data analysis, promote smoother knowledge exchange between different departments, quickly breaking down information silos. Automated analyses and precise resource control ensure proactive and efficient collaboration, accelerating the transition from individual creativity to collective intelligence within the company. In such an environment, the potential of knowledge resources is fully realized, scaling up the innovation process. However, the widespread use of AI also brings structural issues. Data privacy, algorithmic bias, and technological monopolies pose challenges that directly affect the fairness and transparency of the start-up ecosystem. Ignoring technological ethics could cause potential harm to key stakeholders and exacerbate social inequalities. Therefore, founders need not only entrepreneurial acumen but also balance technological capabilities with social responsibility to embark on more responsible innovation paths. In other words, AI is no longer just a tool for increasing efficiency or optimizing processes but has become a strategic cornerstone of innovation systems. In this context, resilient entrepreneurship is characterized by founders' ability to effectively coordinate technological and human resources and continuously create value in complex and dynamic markets. The future success of start-ups will largely depend on how they master AI technologies and use them to shape sustainable innovation systems in a rapidly changing business environment. This requires the next generation of founders to have the ability for overarching integration, with AI as the core technology, to advance collaboration between technology, management, and social values.

The Significance of AI for the Start-Up Scene

Rapid changes in the global economy and technological progress are driving profound changes in the start-up ecosystem. AI is a revolutionary technology that paves unprecedented paths for entrepreneurs. It not only creates new market opportunities through data analysis and automation but also helps reduce uncertainties in the start-up process, enabling high-quality and scalable decision-making.

This section explores how AI accelerates the start-up life cycle through data-driven support, automation tools, and resource concentration. From market research to optimizing business operations, AI is transforming the start-up ecosystem comprehensively but also brings technical and social challenges.

How AI Transforms Start-Up Methods

With powerful algorithms and data processing capabilities, AI significantly expands the application scope of start-up tools. Traditional tools are often limited by the scalability and analysis speed of human capabilities, while AI can process complex data in-depth and multidimensionally, providing entrepreneurs with smarter strategies and tactics.

Precise Market Segmentation and Demand Identification

AI integrates big data on user behavior with ML models, enabling entrepreneurs to conduct market segmentation and demand forecasting with maximum efficiency. For example, entrepreneurs can use AI tools to analyze consumer preferences based on social media interactions, shopping habits, and search histories, and even identify hidden needs.

Case: Discovering Untapped Market Segments

A food-tech start-up analyzed global consumer behavior in the plant-based food sector using AI. By identifying keyword trends, sentiment analysis in comments, and sales data, AI uncovered an underestimated market potential for "high-protein plant-based snacks." The company subsequently launched a protein product and quickly attracted a large number of first-time buyers.

In such scenarios, the value of AI lies not only in accelerating market analysis but also in reducing subjective errors. Compared to traditional methods, AI provides a dynamic, timely, and global perspective, enabling entrepreneurs to act agilely and strategically.

Data-Driven Product and Business Model Adjustment

AI not only aids in analysis but also directly participates in the design of products and business models. Using historical data, AI can develop predictive models that help entrepreneurs create comprehensive and optimized business plans. Advanced analysis tools can offer improvement suggestions based on variable relationships, thereby reducing resource waste.

Case: Optimizing Subscription Services with AI

A fitness app start-up used AI to analyze the behavior of subscribers and cancellers and adjusted its subscription service. By identifying the most common reasons for cancellations and the most important customer interaction points in the subscription life cycle, the company implemented targeted incentive measures. This increased the customer retention rate by 30%, which immediately had a positive impact on revenue.

AI's ability to optimize business operations not only provides entrepreneurs with data-driven insights but also reduces reaction time to market changes.

Automation and Intelligent Task Allocation

From repetitive tasks to optimizing entrepreneurial resources, AI is revolutionizing the efficiency of start-ups through automation. Entrepreneurs can employ AI-supported customer service systems or smart contracts for automated supply chain execution.

Practical and Cost-Effective AI Applications

An e-commerce start-up integrated AI into its order system to automate processes such as customer service requests, inventory updates, and logistics tracking using NLP and computer vision. This reduced labor costs by 40% and cut processing time by over 50%, freeing up more resources for the team to focus on product innovation.

This simple automation application demonstrates the immediate benefits of AI in improving start-up efficiency, especially in the resource-intensive early stages.

AI-Driven Network and Ecosystem Management

In today's highly collaborative entrepreneurial landscape, AI is not just an autonomous tool; it also promotes the integration of resources through network effects, such as by establishing cross-industry partnerships. Open AI development platforms and data-sharing ecosystems enable even small start-ups to access top-tier resources.

Building an Intelligent Start-Up Ecosystem

A start-up accelerator based in Silicon Valley has employed AI to realize "intelligent incubation." An AI-supported matching platform quickly identifies technical partners, investors, and target customers based on the specific needs of start-ups. This not only reduces information asymmetry in resource searching but also enhances the utilization efficiency of these key resources.

The network effect facilitated by AI will further maximize the synergy potential of start-up resources, enabling founders to achieve breakthroughs even with limited resources.

How AI Reduces the Risk of Start-Up Failures

Although entrepreneurship is inherently risky, AI tools can help predict risks and develop proactive measures to transform potential failures into manageable challenges.

Comprehensive Risk Analysis

AI-supported tools can predict environmental changes across multiple dimensions, from economic policy factors to market demand fluctuations and competitive dynamics. For example, specific AI models can monitor real-time data to identify supply chain risks and propose dynamic solutions.

Global Supply Chains: Practical Application of an AI Early-Warning System

A cross-border e-commerce company implemented an AI-based supply chain monitoring system. During the global pandemic, the AI detected potential disruptions in the supply chain in certain markets early on. This enabled the company to quickly switch to alternative suppliers and also stockpile materials in advance, thereby avoiding interruptions and bringing the company a higher cash flow and additional profits. In contrast, competitors faced financial difficulties due to supply problems.

Intelligent Financial Management

Especially cash flow optimization is one of the central challenges for start-ups. AI-supported financial management tools help founders to use capital more efficiently. Intelligent algorithms can dynamically adjust budgets based on real-time data and offer personalized financing suggestions.

Practical Application of a Financing Tool

A start-up in the field of AI for medical technology used an AI-supported planning tool that developed a personalized financing strategy and outlined the optimal investment cycle for research and expansion. The tool also connected the company with three venture capitalists, thereby improving both the negotiation position and capital efficiency.

How AI Shapes the Future of Entrepreneurship

In the AI-driven entrepreneurial environment, AI-based tools are increasingly becoming key factors for success. In the future, these tools may integrate more interdisciplinary technologies, such as blockchain and emotional computing, to provide more diverse and intelligent support. However, with the expansion of AI, new challenges also arise, including potential technological dependence and the risk of neglecting human-centered leadership aspects.

The most successful founders will be those who not only deeply integrate AI tools but also remain sensitive to human needs and values during the integration process. They utilize the acceleration provided by AI without losing sight of the strategic direction.

Conclusions and Insights

AI-supported tools for businesses offer founders more opportunities and capabilities in a cost-effective manner. However, AI remains just a means, its full potential is only realized when technology, strategy, and human creativity work together to strengthen each other. Against this backdrop, the primary goal of innovators remains unchanged: to meet the needs of society with the best solutions.

Founders need not only the opportunity to follow the AI trend but also the ability to gain in-depth insights from the technology that align with their visions. Only in this way can AI become a driving force for success rather than a detour away from the intended goals.

2.15 Innovation Labs: The AI-Powered Innovation Engines

In the context of global economic competition and accelerated technological change, the survival and growth of companies are increasingly determined by innovation. The renewal of thinking and practice requires a redesign of the technology ecosystem.

AI is the central driving force of this new era, helping companies fundamentally transform their innovation methods.

The New Innovation Paradigm in the Age of AI

Corporate innovation labs serve as ideal platforms in this process. By integrating AI, not only is the agility of research and development processes enhanced, but also the ability to explore new, previously uncharted areas is expanded. With the help of AI, innovation labs and downstream development departments can reduce development costs and optimize the speed of market validation, thereby responding precisely and quickly to global competition.

This section explores how AI permeates various levels of innovation labs to provide companies with competitive advantages. It also analyzes the central challenges of this model to deliver effective guidelines for the next phase of technological practice and commercialization.

Innovation Labs: Concept and Operation

Innovation labs are bridges between cutting-edge technologies and market applications. Their main task is to solve complex problems through interdisciplinary collaboration by integrating internal resources and connecting with external technology and knowledge networks. Unlike traditional research and development departments, innovation labs operate more flexibly, promote openness, and encourage rapid experimentation. The integration of AI leads to qualitative progress in the following areas:

Data-Driven Dynamics: Real-time capture and analysis of large-scale, diverse data sources for quick adjustments of research directions.

Experimental Model Validation: Generation of solutions through AI tools, conducting smaller experiments, and reducing the possibility of errors.

Redefinition of Collaboration Models: AI optimizes teamwork between different functions and provides systematic solutions for complex challenges.

Against this background, innovation labs are transforming from pioneers of technology research to leaders of market transformation with the integration of AI.

How AI Catalyzes the Innovation Potential of Labs

Precise Market Insights and Commercial Validation

AI significantly enhances the ability of labs to capture and respond to market trends. With the help of NLP and ML algorithms, AI analyzes data from customer feedback, competitor movements, and market policy changes. This is done objectively and dynamically to quickly identify market opportunities and potential risks.

Example: A fashion company used the innovations of its AI-supported lab to analyze social media trends and develop fashionable products tailored to the tastes of specific consumer groups. Compared to traditional marketing models, the success rate of product promotion increased by more than 30%.

This data-driven innovation method not only accelerates the validation of new product concepts but also optimizes the path to commercialization. It expands the value of the lab from "early exploration" to "comprehensive life cycle management."

Agile Development Through Generative AI Technologies

Generative AI models (such as large language models and image generation algorithms) have become central tools for rapid development and iteration in labs. Unlike traditional product development, where the creation of prototypes or documentation takes a lot of time, AI can quickly deliver numerous creative ideas and prototypes.

Example: Rapid Prototyping: An automotive company's innovation lab used an AI-supported design platform to significantly shorten development cycles. The AI created and tested several vehicle interfaces in the shortest possible time, ultimately leading to the successful market launch of a multifunctional display system.

This agile development is characterized by two main features: First, high flexibility in experimentation, which significantly reduces the costs of failures in concept validation. Second, improved integration of different disciplines, with seamless combination of data technology and product design, significantly enhancing interdepartmental collaboration.

Building Knowledge Platforms to Solve Information Silos

The effectiveness of innovation labs depends not only on advanced tools but also on efficient collaboration within teams and resources. AI-driven knowledge management systems solve this problem and achieve the following goals:

Automatic structuring of numerous documents to transform them from unstructured data into user-friendly information.

Creation of knowledge graphs that enable lab groups to connect past research results and technical documents.

Intelligent recommendations that promote interactions between different team members within an information silo.

Example: The innovation lab of a medical device manufacturer implemented knowledge graph-based AI technology to access cross-departmental past research data and identify rarely used models. This optimized a stalled project, resulting in significantly improved financial and social outcomes.

Artificial Intelligence Innovation Labs: Advantages, Challenges, and Future Prospects

Advantages: The Innovation Lever of Artificial Intelligence

Forward-Looking Technology Identification

With the help of AI-supported predictive models, labs can identify future market demands and competitive changes in advance. For example, AI simulates the impacts of political changes in real time, enabling companies to flexibly respond to macroeconomic shifts.

Cost Optimization

The traditional high costs of research and development as well as lengthy experimental time spans have been significantly reduced by AI. For instance, in the energy sector, some labs have used AI to simulate the physical properties of various materials, eliminating the need for months of physical experiments and thereby conserving resources.

Long-Term Competitiveness

AI strengthens companies' ability to continuously adapt to changes. Labs not only contribute to current innovation but also ensure sustainable competitiveness in dynamic markets through data storage and continuous optimization of models.

Challenges in Applying AI in Innovation Labs

Despite the powerful tools that AI offers, there are several key challenges in its implementation. The most important two are:

High Specialization and the "Black-Box" Effect Problem

The use of AI requires highly qualified interdisciplinary specialists. However, the complexity of algorithms and the opaque nature of model training can lead to teams overly relying on AI results for decision-making without questioning the underlying logic.

Solution: Creating "AI Explanation Expert" roles within the lab team and involving third parties to regularly audit algorithms to ensure their reliability and transparency.

Ethical Issues and Data Privacy Conflicts

AI-supported labs often use extensive datasets, and improper handling of these can lead to ethical and privacy issues.

Solution: Introducing clear data privacy protocols and transparent processes, and enhancing data encryption and traceability to balance efficiency and legality.

Future Outlook: Comprehensive Innovation for Social Challenges

The next step for innovation labs should go beyond mere profit increase. They should actively work on using AI to tackle broader social issues such as environmental protection, medical equity, and urbanization. By collaborating with governmental organizations and NGOs, AI-supported labs can create a platform for in-depth technological development.

In the future, the success of a lab will not only be measured by how much it increases corporate profits but also by its ability to balance technological progress with the interplay of commercial and social benefits. This poses a profound test for all participants in the innovation process.

Conclusion

AI is evolving from a tool to a core pillar of innovation labs. It significantly enhances research speed, resource management, and market responsiveness. Despite existing challenges, the key lies in the strategic use of technology, optimization of governance mechanisms, and expansion of cooperation boundaries. AI innovation labs will not only lead the future of technological research but also create new possibilities for sustainable global development.

2.16 Knowledge Management and Collaboration Platforms

In an environment of continuous technological progress and intense global competition, the success of a company increasingly depends on the effective management and enhancement of its internal knowledge. Traditional knowledge management approaches, such as isolated data storage and fragmented collaboration tools, often prove to be the biggest obstacles to agile innovations. Knowledge management and collaboration platforms are supposed to tear down information silos to unleash innovation potential.

Redefining the Driving Force of Corporate Innovation

The rise of AI paints a completely new picture of knowledge management and collaboration by connecting the flow of information, unleashing the potential of teams, and enabling companies to stay at the forefront of complex markets.

This section highlights the central role of AI in building intelligent knowledge management and collaboration platforms and examines the key functions, practical applications, and potential challenges in this area to provide companies with practical references for successfully dealing with changes.

The Dilemma of Information Silos and the Breakthrough Through AI

Information Silos: The Hidden Costs in Organizations

In companies, information silos refer to the barriers between different departments, teams, or technologies that hinder the flow of information. This problem not only leads to a decline in productive efficiency but also stifles the internal innovation power of the organization. An example is a scenario where archived business data from the finance department could provide valuable insights for marketing decisions but is ignored due to system incompatibilities or lack of semantic connections.

The existence of information silos poses a significant constraint on innovation, the consequences of which are not only seen in redundant work and resource waste but also in weakened capabilities for knowledge reuse and strategic decision-making.

Artificial Intelligence: The Bridge Between Knowledge and Value

The core advantage of AI lies in its extraordinary ability to process data and gain insights. With technologies such as NLP, ML, and knowledge graphs, AI can systematically eliminate information silos:

Semantic Analysis: AI can extract key information from unstructured data (such as documents, logs, or internal business communications) and automatically classify and archive data.

Knowledge Linking: By building knowledge graphs that integrate different departments and structures, AI creates a central knowledge platform with context-related relationships.

Intelligent Decision Support: Real-time data analysis provides precise assistance, including optimization of resource allocation, market trend predictions, and risk analysis scenarios.

This modern transformation significantly enhances a company's control over its knowledge resources, enabling them to be used automatically and intelligently to unleash their full potential.

AI-Supported Collaboration Platforms: Igniting the Innovation Engine

Technical Examples of Cross-Domain Collaboration

Whether it is the development of new products or the shaping of emerging market strategies – cross-domain collaboration forms the core of modern corporate innovation. Traditional collaboration systems, however, often prove to be inefficient due to fragmented technology tools and limited communication channels. AI-supported collaboration platforms solve these problems by creating a unified, coordinated, and intelligent environment:

Seamless Data Integration: AI connects ERP systems, data analysis tools, and project management platforms of companies through API (Application Programming Interface) integration, enabling cross-domain linking.

Intelligent Resource Allocation: AI analyzes task requirements and team members' capabilities to dynamically assign the right people to the appropriate positions, increasing the flexibility of team collaboration.

Optimized Real-Time Collaboration: For global companies, AI supports precise multilingualism, coordination of time-spanning tasks, and efficient interaction between teams of different cultural backgrounds.

An example is an aircraft manufacturer that significantly shortened the design time for the next generation of aviation technology using an AI-supported collaboration platform while avoiding communication problems and redundant design work caused by them.

The Closed Innovation Loop

AI collaboration platforms not only enhance communication efficiency within teams but also create a closed innovation loop; starting from the identification of needs, through their implementation and validation, to the integration of user feedback. Companies can thus build a "Knowledge-as-a-Service" (KaaS) model that efficiently captures market developments and offers direct reactions to them. This agile innovation approach is particularly suitable for fast-paced consumer technology industries as well as individual production.

Knowledge Graph Technology: Creating the Knowledge Map for Companies

Knowledge Graphs: From Fragmented Data to Holistic Information

Knowledge graphs are a data-driven modeling tool supported by AI that connects dispersed knowledge to build a semantic network that reveals hidden relationships and decision-making insights. For example, a retail company used knowledge graphs to identify inefficient processes in its supply chain and shortened delivery times by 15%.

The key features of knowledge graphs include:

Multidimensional Data Integration: The seamless linking of historical data, real-time data, and external market information.
Logical Inference Frameworks: Supporting decision-making by extracting solution paths from complex data structures, such as forecasts for seasonality and demand peaks.
Deeper Semantic Linkages: Discovering new value potentials by analyzing hidden logical connections within data.

Example: Intelligent Integration of Research Data: A globally operating pharmaceutical company used knowledge graph technology to connect internal research data on active ingredients with external studies. This enabled the faster identification of potential combination medications and significantly accelerated decision-making processes. Such intelligent knowledge linkages not only prevent research results from "sinking" but also establish them as the main driver for continuous innovation.

Three Key Technologies for Modernizing Knowledge Management

1. NLP and Intelligent Response Systems
   NLP technologies enable companies to automate the processing of unstructured data. From analyzing customer satisfaction to interpreting contract texts, NLP enhances the efficiency of information processing. Intelligent response systems replace manual inquiries and support developers in efficiently solving complex problems. AI-based assistants can reduce problem-solving time by up to 30%.
2. Semantic Search and AR
   Semantic search options, supported by AI, replace traditional keyword searches and allow employees to retrieve information without exact expertise. Combined with AR, decision aids or instructional materials can be visualized and made directly accessible. For example, in manufacturing, AR can directly display maintenance steps without employees having to search through documentation.
3. Blockchain and Knowledge Security
   Blockchain can secure trust in data transfers and ensure the transparency of knowledge exchanges. Records of knowledge transfer simplify both rights management and innovation projects at the inter-organizational level.

Strategies for Achieving Universal Knowledge Exchange

Development of a Company-Specific Knowledge Exchange Index

AI-generated indicators can optimize the availability, exchange, and reuse of knowledge within companies and strategically utilize it.

Building Dynamic Learning Environments with AI

The development of platforms that update training content in real time promotes employees' quick adaptation to new technologies and applications. For example, Amazon uses an AI-based platform to provide position-relevant training to employees and optimizes content based on learning outcomes.

Promoting Open Cooperation Between Organizations

Companies should conduct experiments with research institutes, universities, and start-ups. AI can simplify the integration of external knowledge sources and uncover deficiencies, an approach that accelerates innovative cycles.

Conclusion: Shaping Intelligent Knowledge Management Systems for the Future

AI-driven knowledge management and collaboration platforms are not only effective tools for optimizing internal corporate resources but also shape a new organizational architecture for the future. Knowledge management becomes a dynamic and self-optimizing ecosystem that enables innovation and strategic development in ways previously unknown.

However, it is clear that organizational intelligence is more than just technical modernization. It is about establishing a human-centered, collaborative, and holistic approach to development through technological progress, for the success of companies but also for the meaningful integration of technology into everyday and professional life.

2.17 Legal Issues and Contract Review

The deep integration of AI also redefines the fundamental practices in the field of law and compliance, leading to comprehensive improvements in efficiency, accuracy, and decision-making. Through deep learning and NLP, AI systems can quickly process large amounts of legal information, such as contract reviews, regulatory analyses, and document organization, which significantly reduces working hours and the error rate of manual inputs. This efficiency boost is particularly remarkable in complex areas of regulations and supports companies in creating more transparent compliance systems while allowing legal professionals to focus on more strategically valuable activities.

Intelligent contract analysis tools have now become central elements of legal work. These tools mark potential legal risk points and contradictory clauses using algorithms, allowing problems in contracts to be quickly identified. They enable lawyers to focus on essential content. These optimizations also accelerate negotiation processes between companies, making their operations and cooperation more efficient and transparent. Moreover, rule- and algorithm-based review capabilities offer the advantage of more precise comparisons and changes in complex contract clauses, surpassing the consistency of manual reviews.

In addition, AI opens up new possibilities in dispute resolution and prediction. By comprehensively modeling and analyzing past case data, AI can predict possible judgments and help legal departments develop more precise strategies for dispute resolution and court proceedings. AI tools can identify key facts and provide data-driven support to give judges and lawyers targeted insights, including case similarity analyses and dynamic monitoring of legal developments. This brings data-driven precision and forward-looking capabilities into legal practice.

In a globalized economy where companies are increasingly active across borders, compliance with regulatory requirements has become a central challenge in compliance management. AI systems can not only monitor in real time how well corporate practices align with legal requirements but also detect anomalies and provide preventive alerts, significantly reducing compliance risks. Particularly noteworthy is the ability of these systems to dynamically integrate differences in regulations between countries, thereby easing the burden of compliance for companies in a global context.

However, AI still requires improvements in terms of context sensitivity, model fairness, and data privacy protection when interpreting regulations, both in technical design and governance mechanisms.

Opportunities and Risks

Despite the great opportunities that AI offers in the field of law and compliance, numerous challenges arise in practical implementation. On the one hand, algorithmic limitations in handling legal content with strongly implied meanings and complex contextual references can affect the reliability of results. On the other hand, the need for transparency and accountability of AI systems emphasizes the necessity to ensure the trust of legal practitioners and clients in the outcomes of AI. In combination with the in-depth experience of legal experts, future intelligent legal systems must be further developed toward human-centered, ethically responsible, and technologically efficient models to fundamentally transform the way of working and the value chain in the legal field.

Redefining Contract and Document Processing

AI fundamentally redefines the processes by which companies handle contracts and documents. Through the use of technologies such as NLP, ML, and other advanced approaches, review efficiency is significantly improved, error rates are reduced, and legal as well as business risks are effectively minimized. These technological advancements not only optimize traditional contract review methods but also expand the application possibilities of contract management tools in complex business environments.

This chapter analyzes the in-depth application of AI in document review and intelligent contract analysis from the perspectives of technological capabilities, practical use cases, industry-specific obstacles and solutions, and future development trends.

Key AI Technologies in Contract Analysis

Natural Language Processing (NLP)

The language in contracts is often highly specialized and strongly structured. During review and analysis, NLP technology can specifically extract key information and perform semantic analysis, thereby increasing the precision and efficiency of contract review. Particularly for long and complex contracts, NLP can automatically categorize essential clauses and conditions, reducing manual effort.

Practical applications of NLP include:

Extraction of Key Conditions: Automatic identification of important content such as payment terms, liability regulations, and choice of law clauses.

Semantic Analysis and Clause Conflict Assessment: NLP analyzes the semantic context and identifies logical inconsistencies in clauses.

Generation of Contract Summaries: Automatic creation of a summary of the main structures and key elements of a contract to provide decision-makers with a quick overview.

Annotation of Legal Entities: Localization of amounts, dates, and party information to support structured data capture of contracts.

Machine Learning and Predictive Models

ML can train models based on extensive historical data that are suitable for predictions and risk assessments. These models identify potential problems or anomalies in contract clauses and help minimize legal risks due to faulty conditions. Moreover, continuous learning constantly improves the accuracy and applicability of contract analysis.

Specific ML technologies include:

Anomaly Detection: Models identify unusual clauses or risky language to uncover hidden problems early.

Risk Assessment: AI analyzes past dispute data to assign numerical risk assessments to contract clauses, supporting negotiation strategies.

Adaptive Rule Application: Optimization of review rules for specific business areas or industry types.

Optical Character Recognition (OCR)

Many contract documents in companies exist as scans or in unstructured formats, making their analysis difficult. The Optical Character Recognition technology converts these documents into structured digital formats that serve as the basis for NLP and ML analyses.

Document Digitization: Rapid processing of PDF or image files to extract key information and compare it with historical contract data.

Error Correction: Automatic correction of recognition errors caused by varying scan qualities to enhance analysis quality.

Application Scenarios: From Contract Review to Comprehensive Decision-Making Support

Risk Assessment and Clause Review

AI-supported contract review systems can quickly identify risks such as unfair clauses or vaguely worded liability regulations. These capabilities are particularly important in cross-border transactions, complex financial arrangements, and long-term service contracts, helping companies avoid legal disputes or financial losses due to contract loopholes.

Example: A global financial services provider implemented an AI tool for contract analysis that marks potential risks in payment clauses and creates detailed risk reports to support negotiation strategies. After its introduction, the processing time for contracts was reduced by 60%, and compliance was significantly improved.

Automation of Contract Review Processes

Traditional review processes require a significant amount of time and labor. AI technology can automate and standardize this process. AI can efficiently compare contract texts with review templates, detect data anomalies, and increase operational security.

Example: A large retail company uses AI to automatically review supplier contracts. The system compares clauses, values, and conditions in real time to ensure the accuracy of the recorded data. After its introduction, review efficiency tripled, and the data error rate decreased by more than 20%.

Review for Compliance with International Regulations

With the globalization of business processes, companies have to deal with complex compliance requirements from different legal jurisdictions. AI tools can efficiently compare contract clauses with current law by integrating legal databases and updating them in real time, avoiding unnecessary risks.

Example: An international biotechnology company used AI to review contracts with data protection clauses to ensure compliance with the General Data Protection Regulation (GDPR). Within 6 months, the system reviewed over 5,000 contracts and significantly shortened the response time of the legal team.

Intelligent Corporate Decision-Making

AI can not only serve as a tool for risk analysis and generating insights from contract data but also actively support corporate decision-making. For example, AI can analyze thousands of old contracts to determine the best combinations of business clauses and optimize negotiations.

Industry Challenges and Solutions

Data Privacy and Compliance

Contracts often contain highly sensitive information, such as financial data, intellectual property agreements, and strategic partnerships. AI systems must ensure that data is protected from misuse or leaks during use.

Solutions: Use advanced encryption algorithms to increase data security when storing contract data. Implement privacy-preserving computing frameworks to protect sensitive data during analysis.

Technical Limitations and Limited Legal Interpretation Capabilities

In semantic analysis of contracts, AI may not be able to reach the depth of human legal experts. For example, clauses with strong contextual associations or specific commercial intentions may be difficult for AI to interpret.

Solutions: Use a collaborative review approach: AI efficiently analyzes simple content, while legal experts focus on complex issues. Develop specialized semantic models to enhance AI's ability to analyze industry-specific contracts.

High Entry Barriers for Small and Medium-Sized Enterprises (SMEs)

Many SMEs do not have the technical or financial resources to deploy complex contract systems.

Solutions: Promote simple Software-as-a-Service (SaaS) solutions based on subscription to provide affordable contract management tools for SMEs. User-friendly design and simplified implementation processes lower entry barriers.

Future Trends and Industry Outlook

Integration of Generative AI

In the future, platforms for contract review and analysis will increasingly integrate generative AI functionalities. This will not only support contract creation but also enable real-time optimization of clauses during negotiation phases and automatic monitoring of contract execution.

Intelligent Cross-Domain Collaboration

AI-supported contract analysis tools will evolve into cross-domain collaboration platforms. These systems will integrate with CRM and ERP systems to enable seamless contract management from creation to execution.

Industry-Specific Solutions

As technologies continue to advance, contract management systems will become more tailored to specific industries. Examples include risk-based frameworks for cross-border trade or customized tools for reviewing IP contracts (intellectual property) for technology companies.

Interim Conclusion

AI technologies are revolutionizing contract review and document management by significantly enhancing efficiency and risk control, moving the entire industry toward a data-driven and intelligent approach. By bridging the gap between technological solutions and human expertise, AI supports companies in shaping their business practices to be secure and compliant in complex environments and building a future-oriented intelligent contract management system.

Litigation Prediction and Case Analysis

The legal field is undergoing a profound transformation driven by technological empowerment. AI as a central force redefines the traditional boundaries of litigation strategies, judgment predictions, and case analyses. Through its ability to process data and model intelligently, AI evolves from a mere tool to an intelligent decision advisor. It helps legal practitioners optimize solution approaches, minimize risks, and promote a transparent and efficient administration of justice.

Shaping the Future of Legal Decisions

The rise of litigation prediction and case analysis not only resolves long-standing information bottlenecks in the legal field but also opens new perspectives for promoting judicial fairness and outcome transparency. From data models to strategy output, AI reshapes the underlying logic of legal services.

What Is Litigation Prediction? Core Values and Application Scenarios

Litigation prediction aims to analyze large amounts of legal data systematically using ML models and NLP technologies to derive possible judgment outcomes, risk levels, and cost assessments. Its core value lies not only in enhancing efficiency and accuracy in litigation forecasting but also in providing scientifically grounded, argumentative support for strategy optimization for legal practitioners.

Application Scenario 1: Analysis of Judgment Trends
The process of judicial decision-making is not a singular decision event but is subject to the interplay of historical data, regional legal culture, and trends in previous judgments. AI analyzes similar past cases to generate comprehensive judgment predictions. An example is an American AI analysis tool for property rights violations. It aggregates data from thousands of judgments and combines contextual information on "judge preferences," "complexity of the legal dispute," and "consistency of witness statements" to achieve over 75% accuracy in predicting judgment probabilities, a valuable aid for lawyers in choosing mediation strategies.

Application Scenario 2: Risk Assessment in the Legal Field
Companies particularly use AI for the initial assessment of legal risks and costs. For example, AI can quickly identify risk-sensitive clauses in disputes over supply chains or labor law disputes and predict the most likely outcomes. A global pharmaceutical conglomerate used an AI-supported risk modeling tool to map its historical case studies in a compliance index, identifying risky areas worldwide and thus avoiding potential multimillion-dollar fines.

Application Scenario 3: Research of Legal Cases and Regulations
Beyond litigation forecasting, litigation prediction significantly accelerates the efficiency of research on relevant legal cases and regulations. Traditional research tools often rely on simple keyword matching, while AI provides deeper insights into the context of cases and justifications through semantic analyses. A major European law firm was able to increase precision in complex case matching by over 40% using an AI tool and reduced the working time of their lawyers to one-third of the original duration. This gives them more room for strategic thinking.

Technological Analysis of Data Modeling in Legal Cases

The prerequisite for intelligent litigation forecasting by AI is accurate and multidimensional data modeling. This process includes not only the challenging interpretation of legal language but also the dynamic inclusion of case context and simulation of possible future factors. The main modeling phases and their technical key points are listed below.

Data Collection and Data Management

The first step in AI modeling is the collection and cleaning of large amounts of legal data, including public judgments, legal regulations, and contract texts. Due to different formats and data opacity, data management is particularly important here. Modern legal technologies combine OCR with multimodal analysis methods to transform structured and unstructured data into inputs suitable for analysis models.

Two key technologies are worth mentioning here: First, cloud-based distributed data collection through legal and compliant data collection from public court sources of different countries. And second, the decryption of restricted agreements from the analysis of encrypted or format-limited legal and business documents.

Legal Semantics and Construction of Knowledge Graphs

Legal texts are highly complex, demanding linguistic precision and consideration of multiple contextual levels. AI leverages NLP to extract semantic information and combines it with domain-specific knowledge to construct knowledge graphs in the legal field.

Technical Application Examples

Named Entity Recognition (NER)

Automatic identification of key units (e.g., case numbers, names of litigants, and amount in dispute).

Legal Ontology Construction

Building case networks that analyze and link related judgments, central evidence, and court rulings.

Model Training and Prediction Optimization

Prediction algorithms are based on both supervised learning methods and deep learning approaches. While the former is trained using specifically labeled cases and templates, neural networks utilize historical data patterns to support complex case predictions.

A critical point in model training is the creation of realistic and trustworthy data labels. For example, in environmental litigation, the amount of damages can vary greatly; thus, the model must accurately predict damage frequencies to avoid ignoring extremes.

AI Assistance in Solving Complex Legal Disputes: A Case Example

In a well-known case of pharmaceutical liability, the plaintiff sued a pharmaceutical company, claiming that its products had led to several health issues and demanded substantial compensation. In traditional court proceedings, analyzing thousands of reports and precedent cases would have taken several months. With an AI solution utilizing the following two stages, the process was significantly accelerated.

Case Analysis Stage

The AI system extracted around 100 highly relevant datasets from 400,000 related legal cases and regulatory provisions. It identified that minor regulatory gaps in product labeling existed only in one region. Given their limited impact, these risks were rated as moderate.

Strategy Development Stage

Reports indicated an 87% likelihood of settlement out of court. The company immediately decided to initiate a negotiation strategy, keeping the compensation under US$5 million, far below potential court rulings.

By employing intelligent case management, the company reduced the time costs of the legal proceedings by at least 70% and significantly enhanced market confidence during the dispute phase.

Challenges in Application: Risks of AI in Legal Practice

Despite the efficiency and potential of litigation prediction, the practice faces several technical, ethical, and legal challenges.

Data Bias and Legal Discrimination

AI algorithms can also inherit biases from historical data. Vulnerable population groups that have been disadvantaged in the past may be similarly disadvantaged in AI predictions, endangering the fairness of the outcomes.

Transparency and Explainability

The "black-box" issue of complex learning models is a widely shared concern in the legal field. Without traceable logical steps, it is difficult for lawyers and judges to accept AI recommendations.

Liability Boundaries and Institutional Adaptation

In legal practice, the question arises of who is liable for incorrect predictions or model risks. Over-reliance on AI could diminish practitioners' expertise and create legal uncertainties.

Future Outlook: Intelligent Decision-Making Consultation

The long-term development of AI in the legal field requires both technological and ethical progress to ensure that it acts as a trustworthy "partner" rather than merely a tool.

Enhancement of Explainable Design

Future AI systems must introduce visualization capabilities to help legal practitioners trace judgment logic and enhance transparency in legal work.

Promotion of Interdisciplinary Collaboration

By linking legal and technical knowledge, ecosystems can be created across multiple levels – from case management to intelligent compliance detection. The integration of ERP systems and contract management tools can make legal services fully intelligent.

Regulation of Data Rights and Ethical Aspects

Clear regulations must also be adopted to govern the use of legal data, data privacy, and the boundaries of intelligent judgment, ensuring the protection of fundamental human rights and fairness.

Interim Conclusion

AI endows legal systems with efficiency and insight previously unattainable. Its central role in litigation prediction and case analysis fundamentally changes the forms of legal work. In the future, AI will not only remain a tool in this field but also act as an intelligent advisor to drive industry innovation and promote the establishment of a more transparent, efficient, and fair legal ecosystem. This in-depth integration could mark the beginning of an era of collaboration between law and technology.

2.18 Compliance Auditing to Enhancing Corporate Conformity

Compliance management has evolved into a strategic core for modern businesses. With the increasing complexity of the regulatory environment and the explosive growth of data volumes, the weaknesses of traditional compliance models are becoming more evident, ranging from low efficiency to frequent errors and uncertain regulatory risks. These issues call for fundamental reform. Technologies like AI are changing the way companies deal with compliance challenges from the ground up by opening new avenues for optimizing management efficiency and responsible action.

Challenges of Compliance Management and the Need for Change

In the context of global business activities, companies face the following compliance challenges:

Rapid Changes in Regulations: Different countries and regions frequently adjust tax, data protection, and environmental regulations, making it difficult for companies to update their standards in time and avoid the risk of violations.

Increasing Data Complexity: The business activities of modern companies involve complex and overarching data networks between departments, regions, and systems. Traditional manual processes are unable to effectively process this information.

High Regulatory Risks: Compliance weaknesses can not only lead to substantial fines but also result in reputational damage and trust crises, further increasing risks for companies.

Regional Regulatory Conflicts: Companies operating in multiple legal jurisdictions often face contradictory requirements from various regulations, posing technical challenges to compliance mechanisms.

In this context, the introduction of AI brings fresh air to compliance management. With stronger automation, precision, and real-time capabilities, AI supports companies in managing complexity, optimizing business processes, and reducing risk exposure.

AI-Based Frameworks for Compliance Auditing

AI redefines the logic of compliance management through data processing, information extraction, and dynamic analyses. The following core areas highlight the valuable contributions of AI to compliance:

Automated Monitoring and Detection: AI systems can continuously monitor corporate activities in real time to detect potential compliance issues. For example, AI algorithms can analyze financial transactions to identify suspicious patterns indicative of fraud or money laundering.

Regulatory Content Analysis: AI can process and analyze vast amounts of regulatory content to keep companies updated on the latest changes. NLP enables AI to understand and interpret complex legal texts, ensuring that companies remain compliant with evolving regulations.

Risk Assessment and Mitigation: AI can assess compliance risks by analyzing historical data and identifying trends. ML models can predict potential areas of noncompliance and suggest measures to mitigate these risks proactively.

Intelligent Reporting and Documentation: AI can automate the generation of compliance reports and documentation. This not only saves time but also ensures accuracy and consistency in reporting, which is crucial for audits and regulatory inspections.

Cross-Functional Integration: AI can integrate compliance processes with other business functions such as finance, human resources, and operations. This holistic approach ensures that compliance is not an isolated activity but is embedded in the overall business strategy.

By leveraging these capabilities, AI can transform compliance management from a reactive to a proactive and intelligent process, ultimately enhancing corporate integrity and trustworthiness in the eyes of stakeholders.

Legal Understanding: From Texts to Action Guidelines

With the continuous development of AI technology, NLP capabilities have provided new possibilities for enterprises to understand and monitor complex regulations. Key application scenarios of AI in the field of legal interpretation include:

Extraction of Legal Elements

AI systems can analyze multipage regulatory documents or texts in multiple languages and transform key compliance attributes into concise operational guidelines. For example, in environmental regulations, AI can quickly translate emission limit values into corporate policies; in data protection regulations, AI can translate user data protection requirements into corporate guidelines.

Synchronization of Dynamic Regulations

AI can track global regulatory changes in real time and automatically compare new regulations with existing operational patterns to identify the need for adjustments. For example, pharmaceutical companies use AI to continuously analyze the compliance of international clinical studies to prevent new regulations from causing operational disruptions.

The deep analysis and interpretation capabilities of AI for regulations not only save a significant amount of labor costs but also improve the reaction speed of enterprises to changes.

Anomaly Detection: From Defense to Prediction

The application of AI in the field of anomaly detection is particularly important, especially in financial transactions, contract execution, and supply chain compliance. Typical methods include:

Real-Time Transaction Checking

With the help of ML algorithms, AI can analyze historical transaction data and detect potential money laundering activities, financial anomalies, or fraud indicators in advance. Large financial institutions use AI models to create anti-money laundering filtering mechanisms, increasing the detection rate of suspicious transactions to over 90%.

Early Warning of Improper Behavior

In production processes, contract execution, and data transmission, AI can identify risk points in advance through anomaly pattern monitoring. For example, chemical companies use AI to monitor equipment emission data in real time. Once the legal limit values are exceeded, the system immediately issues an alarm and provides automatic solutions.

Intelligent Compliance Recommendations

The main difference between AI systems and traditional compliance tools lies in their ability to actively learn and generate intelligent recommendations. This enables enterprises to transform from "reactive compliance management" to "strategic compliance management," specifically manifested as:

Generation of Compliance Action Guidelines

AI analyzes multidimensional data to develop customized compliance recommendations. For example, it may recommend replacing certain partners in a supply chain to avoid illegal transactions with high-risk areas.

Efficient Self-Inspection Tools

Some companies use AI tools to automatically check thousands of contract terms or policy documents and quickly determine compliance. Banks use "compliance assessment models" to make risks visible and quantifiable.

Ensuring Visualization and Understandability

As a "transparent black box," AI compliance systems not only provide specific implementation plans but also offer visual explanations of predictions and recommendations. This is crucial for supporting management and external audits and helps to avoid liability conflicts and social damage. The following are some implementation examples.

Successful Application Under the GDPR

An online retail giant faced the strict requirements of the GDPR. By deploying an AI system, the following compliance goals were achieved: First, the automatic classification and tagging of sensitive data for tens of millions of customers; second, the tracking of global data flows between servers with AI data mapping functions to ensure transparency in data usage; and third, the automatic implementation of deletion requests, such as withdrawing all historical data upon a user's request.

This application efficiently improved compliance and saved the company potential fines from EU regulatory authorities.

Risk Forecasting in the Financial Sector

In the financial sector, the accuracy of compliance decisions is closely related to risk prevention. A regional commercial bank used AI technology to predict credit fraud cases in advance and reduced the credit default rate by 20%. The AI system was particularly good at real-time monitoring of credit data and quickly identifying potential problems by recognizing historical fraud patterns.

These examples not only demonstrate the practical utility of AI-based compliance tools but also reveal the main trend toward predictive compliance.

Core Challenges and Optimization Approaches

Despite significant progress in compliance management, the development of AI is still limited by data technology, ethical, and regulatory constraints:

Data Issues

High-quality data is the foundation for every AI model, but some companies lack sufficient understanding of the legality and security of data collection, which may lead to secondary compliance risks.

Ethical Dilemmas

In some cases, AI monitoring of sensitive activities (such as navigation devices or email content) may infringe on the privacy of employees or customers.

Technical Explainability

Many current deep learning algorithms cannot directly explain the results of their models, which may weaken the credibility of their results, especially in legal responsibilities.

Future technological improvements and guideline developments should focus on increasing model transparency and introducing universally applicable standards to ensure the long-term stability of AI applications.

Building a New AI-Supported Compliance System

Modular Specialized Applications: Developing modular compliance tools for specific areas could promote the expansion of AI from analysis to holistic process management.

Autonomous Learning Systems: AI systems could adapt to macroeconomic environments by updating regulatory databases in real time and automatically optimizing audit models to keep pace with sudden regulatory changes.

Integration with Blockchain: Combining AI with blockchain technology could enhance transparency in compliance management. For example, in pharmaceutical tracking, immutable blockchain records could be combined with AI tools for dynamic analysis and optimization of the supply chain.

Call to Action and Conclusion

AI is no longer just a supplement to traditional compliance processes, but is driving the strategic realignment of compliance management. For the mature application of these tools, a solid technological foundation within companies as well as active support from external guidelines is needed. In the future, the increasing collaboration between technology and regulation will not only improve the operational flexibility of companies but also create a more efficient and fair business environment.

Chapter 3
Practical Applications of AI in Medicine and Healthcare

The rapid development of artificial intelligence (AI) technology is accelerating profound changes in various fields, with the ability to transform theoretical research into practical applications becoming increasingly mature. In the medicine and healthcare sector, AI has significantly enhanced the efficiency of treating complex cases and the precision of therapies through intelligent diagnostics, precision medicine, and image processing. This technology not only excels in medical data analysis and disease prediction but also plays a key role in clinical decision support. However, the application of this technology also brings risks such as data privacy violations and ethical controversies, especially in scenarios involving sensitive patient data. Therefore, precise rules must be developed and strictly implemented to align technological innovation with social responsibility.

AI is penetrating the medicine and healthcare sector comprehensively through core technologies such as deep learning, natural language processing (NLP), and computer vision, driving the transformation from traditional to intelligent health systems. In the field of intelligent diagnostics, AI enables the precise identification and classification of disease characteristics by utilizing extensive medical image datasets and advanced algorithms. For instance, AI has been widely applied in the early detection of cancers such as lung and breast cancer, with diagnostic accuracy surpassing that of human doctors in many cases. Moreover, intelligent diagnostic systems significantly reduce treatment times and play a vital role in regions with limited medical resources by enhancing the efficiency and reach of the entire healthcare system. In the realm of precision medicine, AI integrates patients' genetic information, medical histories, and lifestyle data to develop personalized treatment plans. This not only optimizes treatment efficacy but also reduces side effects. Particularly at the intersection of genomics and deep learning, AI has revolutionized the understanding of disease mechanisms and propelled research into rare diseases as well as the development of precisely effective medications. As technology advances, precision medicine is increasingly moving out of the experimental stage to become a widely applicable field of practice, heralding long-term progress in the development of health services. AI also significantly boosts efficiency in medical research. For example, researchers can use machine learning models to analyze historical and current data to dynamically monitor disease spread patterns and optimize prevention strategies. Another exciting application area is drug development, where AI, by integrating omics data and virtual screening technologies, drastically shortens the duration of drug selection and clinical studies. Omics refers to all research areas ending in -omics (e.g., genomics, proteomics, and metabolomics), which are molecular biological analytical methods targeting specific

 | https://doi.org/10.1515/9783112242728-003

groups of biological molecules. It is an umbrella term for research areas such as genomics, proteomics, and metabolomics. During global health crises, AI-assisted screening has proven particularly valuable in accelerating vaccine development. Despite the great potential of AI in healthcare, there are significant challenges in implementation. Issues such as data privacy and the distribution of data ownership rights are becoming increasingly important. Due to the high sensitivity of medical data, the question arises of how to create open and secure data platforms while protecting patient privacy. Other contentious topics include algorithmic bias and model transparency. Especially in significant medical decisions involving survival, ensuring the fairness and explainability of models is crucial. The spread of AI in healthcare also brings ethical challenges, including reshaping professional role distribution and doctor-patient relationships, which requires medical professionals to rethink their roles. Solving these problems requires mutual cooperation between technology and regulation. On the one hand, technologies such as federated learning can be introduced to ensure the security of sensitive data; on the other hand, policy measures and standardizations are needed to regulate the use of AI systems and minimize potential operational risks. In the future, driven by ethical norms, technological innovations, and regulatory progress, AI will be a central force in transforming the healthcare sector. It will shape a smarter and more sustainable vision for global health development by simultaneously promoting efficiency and fairness.

3.1 Advances and Potential of Intelligent Medical Diagnostic Systems

With the growing influence of AI in the medical field, diagnostic standards are undergoing a comprehensive technological transformation. AI systems, based on the processing of large amounts of data and intelligent analysis, provide medical professionals with more efficient and comprehensive diagnostic tools. These tools significantly increase the precision and speed of disease detection. From deep learning in medical imaging to algorithms for early disease detection, leading countries have already made significant progress in the development of intelligent diagnostic systems. However, the true potential of this technology extends far beyond current achievements and requires a collective effort from the entire industry to address central technical and ethical challenges and establish a responsible AI diagnostic system.

How AI is Changing Traditional Medical Diagnosis

Data-Driven Improvements in Insights

Traditional diagnoses often relied on the experience and intuition of individual doctors, which limited their standardizability. AI enables the integration of multimodal data (such as medical images, electronic health records (EHRs), genomic data, and real-time vital signs) to transition from experience-based to data-driven diagnoses. AI diagnostic systems can recognize subtle patterns in large datasets and extract features beyond human perception, significantly expanding the possibilities for disease detection.

Visual Enhancement of Medical Images

In the field of medical imaging, AI has made unprecedented progress thanks to deep learning technologies. For example, in the detection of lung diseases, models based on convolutional neural networks (CNN) can identify small lesions (damaged or altered tissue areas) in X-ray images and automatically mark them visually. Current studies show that AI models achieve much higher sensitivity in the early detection of lung cancer than radiologists. These models could at least serve as second-opinion tools to reduce misdiagnoses and undetected cases.

Electronic Health Records and NLP Integration

Hospitals have a large amount of unstructured data from EHRs, containing valuable information about diagnoses and treatment pathways. NLP algorithms are capable of extracting important content, such as patterns of early-stage chronic diseases or drug side effects, from these texts. Some AI systems have already proven to improve the efficiency of screening for cardiovascular diseases and generate detailed action recommendations for doctors.

Speed and Efficiency throughout the Lifespan

The real-time analysis capabilities of AI enable an unprecedented response speed in healthcare. In acute scenarios such as strokes or coronary events, AI can analyze medical images within seconds and provide initial diagnostic results, significantly improving the precision of the "golden intervention window." This increase in efficiency is particularly important for remote areas and emergency situations.

Technological Breakthroughs in Intelligent Medical Systems

Collaboration Between Deep Learning and Imaging

Deep learning technology continues to sustainably influence innovation in medical imaging and is increasingly evolving from two-dimensional to three-dimensional, from static to dynamic processing layers. Examples of applications include:

Comprehensive Support for Breast Cancer Screening

The latest CNNs assist in analyzing mammography images and model microcalcified lesion structures in terms of their volume and distribution. This allows for a more precise three-dimensional representation of suspicious areas with an accuracy rate of over 95%. Some platforms that integrate physical modeling and AI algorithms already support radiologists in creating personalized treatment plans.

Unified Analysis of Multimodal Imaging

Deep learning technologies are increasingly being used in comprehensive diagnostic sites, for example, by combining MRI (magnetic resonance imaging) and positron emission tomography data. These approaches enable a molecular analysis of disease foci from various perspectives and accurate prediction of metastases, significantly improving tumor monitoring.

Early Disease Risk Prediction

AI goes beyond the diagnosis of existing diseases and plays a central role in health management and disease prevention. For example, some national health projects have already tested the use of machine learning models for risk assessment, such as stroke risk in hypertensive patients. These models evaluate genomic data, lifestyle habits, and clinical histories to comprehensively analyze potential threats to a patient. Dynamic warning systems and intervention models enable proactive healthcare instead of passive reactions.

Urgent Challenges to Be Solved

Fairness and Universal Application

The most pressing bottleneck for AI-assisted diagnostic systems is algorithmic fairness and universal applicability. Due to regional differences in medical standards, the training datasets for AI models are often based on populations from Western countries and large hospitals. As a result, the specific characteristics of patients from Africa, Latin America, and remote regions are frequently overlooked. This inequality significantly hampers the application in various regions. A solution requires diversified data collection, international cooperation, and the improvement of the universal functionality of algorithms, especially in the field of global health care with distinct inter-ethnic requirements.

Data Privacy and Security: The Foundation of Trust

Another significant barrier for AI in medicine is data privacy and security. Medical diagnoses inevitably rely on sensitive patient data, and inadequate regulation can lead to data breaches, ethical conflicts, and misuse. To address this issue, privacy-preserving technologies such as federated learning should be employed, which allows AI models to be trained locally on devices without central aggregation of data. At the same time, strict industry guidelines and transparent regulatory mechanisms should be established to protect the digital rights of patients.

Explainability and Transparency in Decision-Making Processes

The "black box" problem of AI algorithms has not been fully resolved to date. For example, the logic chains used by deep learning AI when generating diagnostic recommendations are often difficult for doctors to understand and are disconnected from their professional expertise. Enhancing the explainability of models is essential for building trust. Researchers are currently developing interactive visualization tools to make the functioning of AI models transparent and enable doctors to understand the basis of diagnoses. This will significantly increase the acceptance and reliance on the systems.

Key Developments for the Future

Holographic Multimodal Diagnostic Systems

Future-oriented AI-driven diagnostic systems will integrate comprehensive health data to create a complete disease profile of the patient. These systems will combine genomic data, real-time heart rate monitoring, and imaging findings to quickly identify potential causes of illness. At the same time, they can integrate external risk factors such as environmental pollution at the place of residence and propose personalized treatment pathways. Holographic diagnostics will be particularly useful for the management of chronic diseases and accurate forecasting of infectious diseases.

Edge AI and Real-Time Medicine

With the support of edge computing, wearable devices will achieve higher intelligent processing capabilities. Emergency medical technicians could use portable AI systems to analyze intubation images or ECG data in real-time without relying on external servers. These real-time diagnostic tools will minimize the risk of network transmission delays or cloud outages.

International Cooperation and Regulatory Frameworks

The global disparities in national medical AI development levels are increasingly recognized and identified as obstacles to technology dissemination. In the future, international cooperation should be strengthened, for example, by introducing global standardized data protocols, unified data labeling methods, and standardized data exchange practices. At the same time, the sharing of public resources should be promoted, such as providing pretrained AI models, to avoid the concentration of medical resources in industrial countries.

Conclusion and Inspiration

Intelligent medical diagnostic systems have the potential to fundamentally revolutionize traditional diagnostic standards in terms of accuracy, speed, and reach. If algorithmic biases and data privacy issues are overcome, multimodal data is integrated, and international cooperation and standardization are advanced, this field could promote global technological progress in the next 5 years. However, the successful implementation and development of AI technology require a close integration with ethical, social, and political factors. Only by finding a balance at the intersection of technology and humanity can a smarter and more equitable health system be created.

3.2 Artificial Intelligence in Genomic Analysis and Precision Medicine

Amid the revolution in human healthcare, precision medicine is striving for a paradigm shift: from “disease-centered” to “patient-centered.” The in-depth analysis of genomic data forms the central engine of this transformation. Faced with the massive and high-dimensional genomic datasets, traditional methods reach their limits in terms of computing power and efficiency. AI, with its interdisciplinary integration capabilities and the impressive potential of deep learning algorithms, rapidly catalyzes the field of genomic analysis and thus provides the essential technological foundation for precision medicine. This section explores how AI expands the application scenarios of genomic data and delves into the academic progress as well as the central conflicts between research and technical implementation.

The AI-Driven Transformation in Genomic Data Analysis

Behind massive genomic datasets lies the principle of unlocking vital secrets of life. However, traditional analysis methods, due to limited algorithmic models, struggle to fully exploit the potential of these data. The application of AI fundamentally changes genomic data processing, from complex bioinformatics to multi-perspective interpretation. This includes functional prediction, identification of epigenetic mechanisms, and modeling of complex systems.

Breakthroughs of Deep Learning in Functional Prediction of Genomic Sequences

Deep learning methods have opened up entirely new avenues for deciphering genomic sequences, especially in identifying functional DNA regions and modeling complex gene interactions. Algorithms enable the transformation of "unused information" into "manageable knowledge."

Detection of Promoters and Regulatory Regions

Deep learning models based on CNNs demonstrate their ability to identify promoter regions of gene expression. For example, the technology DeepBind can locate critical binding sites of DNA and proteins. It shows a superior role in investigating gene expression patterns and epigenetic mechanisms compared to traditional sequence alignment algorithms.

Precise Prediction of Single-Nucleotide Polymorphisms (SNPs)

With specialized algorithms, researchers can predict the effects of point mutations and genomic region variants on disease risks. This enables real-time linking between epigenetic data and phenotypic analyses and revolutionizes the diagnosis of rare diseases by directly associating genetic mutations with clinical symptoms, an innovative approach in designing therapeutic plans.

NLP Technologies for Multidimensional Semantic Analysis of Genomic Data

By employing NLP in AI, "syntactic structures" of genomic data can be created, thereby enhancing the efficiency of utilizing massive genetic databases. Special architectures promote the annotation of genomic functions as well as the extraction of information from publications, boosting the efficiency of knowledge discovery in academic studies. This technology supports the creation of dynamic genetic network models and transforms static descriptions into dynamic predictions.

AI-Driven Personalization in Precision Medicine

The goal of precision medicine is to develop individually tailored treatment plans for each patient based on genomic data, as opposed to the traditional pharmaceutical effect. AI expands the technical possibilities in this field and brings personalized and pinpoint medicine to a deeper level within practical medical applications.

Multi-OMIC Integration for Comprehensive Diagnosis

Single genomic data cannot fully depict diseases. AI's ability to integrate multi-OMIC data significantly expands the diagnostic spectrum in precision medicine. The combination of systems biology and AI enables diagnoses based on multidimensional data sources rather than single-data limitations.

Analysis of Signaling Pathways in Cancer

Supported by deep learning models, researchers can identify critical regulatory networks of tumors from transcriptomic and metabolomic data, thereby defining the optimal anticancer therapies for patients. For example, AI is used to identify correlations between cancer resistance regions and therapeutic targets, which substantially optimizes the design of treatment plans.

Prediction of Individual Therapeutic Outcomes

By combining genetic data, protein data, and environmental factors, AI models can, for example, predict the dynamic effects of treatment plans and thus provide a more precise evaluation of outcomes. For instance, adjusting the dosage of anti-tumor drugs based on a patient's genetic properties enables precise tuning and prevents unnecessary side effects.

Revolutionary Advances in Pharmacogenomic AI

The core task of pharmacogenomics lies in interpreting genetic data to individually determine drug sensitivity for patients, a field where AI delivers revolutionary breakthroughs.

Optimization of Individual Drug Selection and Dosage

Algorithms have begun to develop personalized treatment schemes for high-risk patients based on specific genotypes. These data-driven approaches find application in the development of precise anticancer drugs and significantly enhance clinical efficacy.

Detection of Antibiotic Resistance Mechanisms

With AI-supported models, genetic expression patterns of resistance genes can be efficiently captured, allowing treatment strategies to quickly adapt and prevent the spread of resistance.

Breakthroughs of AI in Diagnosis and Intervention of Genetic Diseases

Genetic diseases pose one of the greatest challenges in traditional medicine. AI provides innovative solutions from causal analysis to therapeutic intervention.

Intelligent Tools for Diagnosing Rare Diseases

Rare genetic diseases have low prevalence and complex data structures. The combination of expert knowledge and AI systems has significantly increased the effectiveness of their diagnosis.

Fusion of Imaging Data and Genetic Diagnosis

Tools like Face2Gene use facial features and clinical indicators to identify potential genetic disease causes, significantly increasing the precision of cause identification.

AI to Expand Genetic Editing Technologies

The development of gene-editing tools like CRISPR is largely limited by unpredictable off-target effects. Deep learning algorithms offer optimization possibilities by simulating potential effects at target sites before editing and reducing distortion risks.

Use Case: Application of AI in Precision Medicine for Breast Cancer

In the context of personalized breast cancer treatment, AI demonstrates an innovative interplay between genomic analysis for DNA sequencing and clinical interventions.

In the revolution of human health care, precision medicine is striving for a paradigm shift, from "disease-centered" to "patient-centered." The in-depth analysis of genomic data is the core driving force of this transformation. Faced with massive and high-dimensional genomic data sets, traditional methods have reached their limits in computing power and efficiency. AI, with its interdisciplinary integration capabilities and the impressive potential of deep learning algorithms, has rapidly catalyzed the field of genomic analysis and provided the necessary technological foundation for precision medicine. This section explores how AI expands the application scenarios of genomic data and delves into the academic progress as well as the core conflicts between research and technical implementation.

Real-Time Tracking of Disease Progression

The OncoAI system combines patients' gene expression data with treatment plans, increasing the prediction rate for postoperative relapse risks to 95%. With deep learning support, the system optimizes the efficiency of anticancer drugs, shortens recovery time, and improves patients' quality of life.

Challenges and Future: The Co-Evolution of AI in Genetics and Precision Medicine

Despite showing tremendous potential, AI still faces several significant challenges. The most important are:

Lack of Data Quality and Representativeness: The unbalanced representation of genomic data affects the adaptability of models, especially in non-representative genetic backgrounds.

Ethics and Data Privacy: The sensitivity of genetic information places high demands on data storage and exchange, requiring robust data privacy mechanisms.

Interpretability of Algorithms: The "black-box" effect of deep learning models limits their comprehensive clinical application. Standardized design criteria for interpretable AI should be promoted. Possible development paths include: First, promoting the standardization and global exchange of genomic databases. Second, integrating human knowledge priorities into algorithmic prediction models. And third, exploring real-time monitoring and dynamic decision-support procedures to make health services more efficient and precise.

Conclusion

With the intensive integration of AI and genomics, the research of precision medicine is moving toward entirely new horizons. Technological progress is guiding medicine from a one-dimensional focus to a multidimensional approach, from individual data to global strategies. AI not only enhances diagnostic and treatment capabilities but also fundamentally changes medicine through the cooperation between technology and human-centered design. Precision medicine could achieve crucial progress on the path to global health equity through the joint efforts of science and ethics.

3.3 Breakthroughs and Validation in Medical Imaging Analysis

With the progress of AI, medical imaging analysis is undergoing a profound transformation that significantly enhances the precision and efficiency of medical diagnostics. From traditional manual image interpretation to AI-assisted interpretation, the superiority and broad application potential of AI in this field are demonstrated. Using technologies such as computer vision, deep learning, and multimodal fusion, AI is fundamentally changing models of medical diagnosis and achieving groundbreaking results in key areas such as cancer screening, cardiovascular disease monitoring, and pathological analysis. This section explores the contradictions and solutions in the implementation of such technologies and examines how AI can contribute to ensuring medical quality and optimizing processes in the long term.

Key Innovations in Imaging Analysis

Deep Learning and Automated Feature Extraction

Deep learning, especially the use of CNN, forms the basis for AI's breakthroughs in medical imaging analysis. Unlike traditional image analysis tools that rely on manually designed feature extraction, AI enables the automatic identification of hidden patterns and features in image data.

In recent years, the ResNet architecture (residual neural networks) has proven particularly effective in addressing the problem of vanishing gradients and improving training efficiency for complex image data by introducing residual connections. U-Net structures (a type of CNN specifically designed for medical image segmentation) have become indispensable for their excellent performance in tumor boundary identification and lesion extraction, especially in cancer diagnosis. Lightweight network architectures like EfficientNet (a family of CNNs) improve computational efficiency, creating conditions for broad clinical application.

Multimodal Imaging Fusion for Comprehensive Diagnostic Capabilities

Disease diagnosis can often be limited by the constraints of individual imaging sources, such as distorted or incomplete information. Multimodal imaging fusion driven by deep learning represents a key advancement. This technique combines data from various imaging sources, such as MRI, CT, X-ray, and ultrasound, to create a comprehensive diagnostic model. For example, in detecting brain tumors, combining MRI data with detailed soft tissue information and CT data with high contrast allows for a more precise description of the affected areas, significantly enhancing diagnostic accuracy.

Optimization through Reinforcement Learning and Automation

Reinforcement learning models are driving the automation of image analysis processes. These algorithms can find the optimal solution for segmentation, lesion localization, and 3D reconstruction through repeated testing and strategic adjustments. In the field of breast cancer screening, the precise detection of hidden microcalcifications by dynamically trained models has proven to be a significant advancement. Moreover, the ability for unsupervised learning opens up new possibilities for detecting diseases with unclear boundaries.

Technical Implementation: Applications of AI in Disease Diagnosis

Cancer Early Detection and Risk Assessment

Early detection of cancer is a key aspect for successful diagnosis and therapy. AI shows particularly promising results in the early detection of breast cancer, lung cancer, and skin cancer. In a recently conducted multicentric study, an AI-supported analysis tool for mammography images achieved a detection accuracy of over 95%. This technology not only reduces the workload for radiologists but also enhances the ability to identify the slightest pathological changes at an early stage.

For example, a hospital developed a deep learning CT analysis tool for lung cancer diagnosis, which not only predicts the size and growth potential of lesions but also provides risk prognoses. By incorporating clinical pathology data, the tool offers concrete scientific support for cause research and therapy planning and adjustment.

Dynamic Monitoring of Cardiovascular Diseases

Dynamic image analysis through AI plays a crucial role in the diagnosis of cardiovascular diseases and enables timely intervention. One of the breakthroughs is an AI application that creates precise models for the localization and marking of lesions from time-staged heart ultrasound and coronary CTA images. An FDA-approved deep learning tool for stroke, for example, identifies thrombi and assesses their severity within minutes. This not only significantly reduces the doctor's decision-making time but also determines the time window for life-saving treatment options.

AI also proves its sensitivity in monitoring vascular anomalies by automatically and precisely extracting flow velocity and blockage information from image data. This makes the technology an indispensable tool in the diagnosis of complex diseases.

Analysis of Tissue Samples and Microscopic Cellular Behavior

The application of AI in pathology enables more efficient and reliable diagnoses. For example, generative adversarial networks and multi-task learning algorithms significantly reduce the error rate in detecting tumor areas in tissue sections. These technologies are not only effective in segmentation but also provide predictive support in determining the size and spread of a tumor (tumor staging).

AI's analysis of dynamic cellular changes at the molecular level finds application in drug development. By tracking cellular behavior when exposed to new drugs, researchers can evaluate their efficacy and potential side effects early on. These approaches accelerate the development of new therapies and increase the efficiency of drug research.

Limits of Technology: Conflicts and Solutions

Biased Data and Limited Generalizability

The performance of AI models strongly depends on the quality and diversity of training data. Current medical image data mostly comes from affluent regions like Europe and North America, limiting its applicability to patients from lower-income countries or Africa and Asia. To address this discrepancy, enhanced international cooperation in data collection and the development of robust, adaptive models are necessary. Federated learning technologies, which enable joint model training without compromising data privacy, offer a promising solution to minimize data biases.

Algorithmic Transparency and Trust Building

The complexity and lack of explainability of deep learning models face criticism in medical practice. The so-called "black-box" diagnostics hinder trust between doctors and patients. Active efforts are aimed at developing explainable AI technologies such as saliency maps, which make decision-making bases visible and highlight them. Hybrid diagnostic approaches that combine the expertise of doctors with algorithmic analyses are also increasingly used.

Data Privacy and Ethical Challenges

The privacy of image data is a crucial factor for the broad acceptance of AI. It is necessary to employ technological developments such as distributed training methods and stronger encryption to ensure security and data integrity. In addition, there is a need for internationally unified ethical standards and legal regulations to ensure compliance with data protection requirements and promote responsible technological development.

Outlook and Inspiration

The rapid development of AI-supported image analysis offers unprecedented opportunities for precision and efficiency in medicine. However, challenges in the areas of technology, ethics, and trust remain. With multimodal fusion, enhanced model explainability, and comprehensive clinical validations, AI has the potential to lead medical image analysis into an intelligent future. It is particularly important that technological innovations are not limited to affluent regions but contribute to optimizing global health systems. In the field of disease diagnosis and resource redistribution, AI will play an increasingly central role and promote cycles of global equality.

3.4 Ethical Challenges and Solutions for Medical Applications of AI

The rapid development of AI is revolutionizing the healthcare industry in unprecedented ways, particularly in terms of efficiency, precision, and reach. However, this technological revolution also brings with it a host of ethical concerns, ranging from the vulnerability of data privacy to the imperfections of algorithmic fairness and the delays in technological inclusivity. Ethical challenges are a key factor limiting the further integration of AI into the medical field. Striking a balance between technological progress and human care requires collective discussion and implementation.

This section examines the ethical challenges of medical AI, analyzes the central contradictions of technological innovation, and proposes feasible solutions to enable sustainable implementation of the technology.

Data Ethics: The Battle for Medical Privacy

The Special Sensitivity of Medical Data

Medical data is significantly different from general information. It includes patients' health conditions, genetic information, and medical histories, all highly sensitive content. On the other hand, training AI models requires large amounts of data, making medical data particularly valuable and susceptible to misuse. Every step in the process, such as labeling, storage, and transmission, can be a potential point of entry for data abuse or privacy violations.

A typical case is an international pharmaceutical company collaborating with medical institutions on AI-assisted drug research. Despite promises of data anonymization, patient information was inadvertently disclosed due to the reconstruction capabilities of algorithms. This raised serious doubts about the reliability of encryption technology.

The Era of Data Security Issues

In recent years, medical institutions have increasingly become targets of cyberattacks. In 2021, a hospital in Virginia, USA, suffered a ransomware attack that exposed over 15 million patient records, almost paralyzing the hospital's operations. This demonstrates that AI in healthcare faces the challenge of fully utilizing data without turning it into a security risk.

The specific issues lie in the following areas: High risks from data centralization, because centrally stored data is particularly vulnerable to attacks. Unclear responsibilities between technology developers and data owners, because companies often have strong control over the use of data without directly managing it. There are inconsistent data protection regulations and different mechanisms for protecting privacy between countries and institutions increase system risks. And last but not least technological approaches for reshaping data protection mechanisms

To address the challenges of data protection and data security, the following technologies and frameworks are gaining increasing importance:

Federated Learning

Federated learning allows model training in multiple local centers without sending data to central servers. This technology significantly reduces the risk of data privacy violations and data misuse. For example, several hospitals collaborated using federated learning to develop AI-assisted cancer screening algorithms without sharing raw data.

Blockchain-Based Data Security Management

Blockchain is known for its tamper-proof nature and can document every step of data usage in the medical field. With this technology, patients can monitor their data usage in real time and revoke authorization at any time. For example, a blockchain-based health data management platform was developed in Sweden.

Differential Privacy

This technology adds random noise to statistical analyses to prevent the tracing of sensitive individual data. Apple uses this technology in its health AI projects to conduct disease trend feedback analysis while ensuring the security of sensitive data.

Ethics of Fairness: The Health Gap for Disadvantaged Groups

The Spread of Algorithmic Bias

Algorithmic bias reflects the shortcomings of training data. In the medical field, these biases can lead to significant inequality. For example, a well-known AI tool for predicting heart disease had an accuracy rate up to 30% lower for African American patients. The reason is that the training data was mainly derived from affluent European populations. This not only violates medical fairness but can also lead to diagnostic delays for already resource-poor patient groups.

Similar situations also occur in diagnostics. In some AI models, women fare worse than men in terms of detection accuracy when fewer image data from women were used in the data creation phase.

The Real Challenges of Technological Inclusivity

The use of AI is mainly concentrated in research centers and hospitals in affluent areas, while remote areas rarely benefit from the technological advantages. Health stations in rural areas often cannot use cloud-based AI diagnostic technology, either due to high hardware costs or inadequate network infrastructure. This resource disparity further exacerbates the inequality in medical care.

Technological Approaches: Constructing a Framework for Fairness and Inclusivity

Strategies for Diverse Data Sampling

It is essential to create multicentric and culturally diverse data sources that ensure large amounts of information, including ethnicity, gender, age, and socioeconomic status, are taken into account. The global alliance for shared patient data promoted by the United Nations could serve as a platform for cooperation.

Algorithmic Adjustments for Fairness

Using sensitivity detection technologies, biased data can be identified and corrected during model training. Studies show that an algorithm with more weight on underrepresented samples can significantly increase accuracy in breast cancer diagnosis. For instance, an AI platform for African patient groups has achieved similarly precise results as for European data.

Innovative Inclusivity Solutions

Developing AI models tailored for low-resource environments, such as simplified versions of AI tools for diagnosing abdominal ultrasound images that can be integrated into local clinics using smartphone hardware and cost only a fraction of traditional devices.

Ethics Governance: Institutional Protection and Shared Responsibility

Establishing Standardized Ethical Guidelines

Ethical issues with AI can only be resolved through standardized rules established collectively by multiple parties:

Governments should enact regulatory guidelines for medical AI, obliging companies to make their decision-making logic and potential risks transparent.

Medical professional associations could introduce a certification system for ethical compliance to ensure that AI tools are legal and regulation-compliant.

Oversight and Transparency by Ethics Committees

Large hospitals and AI development companies could establish internal ethics committees with experts from technology, law, and patient representation to independently review applications. Involving patients in ethical discussions strengthens public trust in the technology.

Education and Public Engagement

Through awareness programs and patient information, the public could be better informed about the benefits and risks of AI in healthcare. For example, a transparency report on studies could be published on public platforms to reduce information asymmetry and promote awareness of ethical issues.

Summary and Outlook

The use of AI in healthcare is increasingly becoming a part of social infrastructure. Ethical questions must not be overlooked. Data privacy, security, fairness, and inclusivity are crucial points for the further progress of AI. The application of modern technological solutions and the creation of a strong ethical framework can help ensure the balance between scientific innovation and social responsibility.

In the next ten years, AI, with its increasing capabilities, will not only be a tool for improving treatment but also a central driving force for medical fairness and health equality. Only when ethical issues are considered an essential part of the agenda can the intelligent medicine revolution truly be comprehensive and far-reaching.

Chapter 4
Affective AI to Understand Emotions

The development of affective artificial intelligence (AI) has made a groundbreaking advance in optimizing human-machine interaction. Its ability to recognize human emotions significantly enhances the adaptability of services. From intelligent customer service to mental health monitoring, this technology constructs more natural and emotionally deeper interaction scenarios for users. However, algorithmic biases in emotion recognition and the potential misuse of sensitive datasets limit its dissemination. This also poses a serious challenge to technical ethics and regulatory guidelines. Therefore, transparency in data sources, proof of algorithmic fairness, and the strict implementation of data protection mechanisms are key prerequisites for the widespread application of this technology.

Affective AI and emotional AI are basically the same field, that focuses on building systems, which can detect, interpret and respond to human emotions. This area revolutionizes the future direction of human-machine interaction through its transformative technological vision. Unlike traditional AI, which focuses on functional efficiency, emotional AI emphasizes the recognition and reaction to emotions to enable more personalized and human interactions. By combining speech analysis, facial expression recognition, and monitoring of physiological signals, emotional AI can dynamically interpret users' emotional states and offer personalized and context-dependent solutions for various scenarios. For example, emotion-driven recommendation systems based on users' current feelings can provide precise suggestions, thereby overcoming the limitations of traditional algorithmic concepts that rely solely on historical preferences. In practice, this technology shows unique potential in various fields.

AI-based emotional assistance systems in the service sector can adjust their tone and strategies in real time to users' emotional fluctuations, thereby increasing customer satisfaction and loyalty. In medical applications, emotional AI can support mental health care by monitoring emotions and helping doctors create personalized treatment plans. Similarly, in the field of education, an intelligent teaching assistant can optimize the learning rhythm and design of interactivity through emotional data, from promoting learning interest to stress management, a significantly improved educational experience is achieved. However, to realize this in-depth integration, emotional AI must overcome technical and ethical challenges. Currently, technical bottlenecks mainly lie in data bias and the robustness of algorithms, especially in multicultural contexts, as different regions and people express emotions in different ways, which often leads to insufficient accuracy in emotion assessment. In addition, the collection and use of emotional data also raise questions of privacy and ethics. It is crucial to find a balance between public transparency and commercial application; this requires active exploration and development of standardized solutions by compa-

 | https://doi.org/10.1515/9783112242728-004

nies and research institutions. These challenges not only involve technical implementation but also have a profound impact on the social acceptance of widespread dissemination. The comprehensive implementation of emotional AI requires interdisciplinary cooperation and transparency in the development process, especially in data security, model optimization, and ethical responsibility. Developers and policymakers are called upon to jointly create standards to reconcile the cultural adaptation needs of algorithms with user data protection. Only through continuous iteration and standardization can emotional AI be widely implemented and open up new dimensions of interfaces for human-machine cooperation.

Language assistants, natural language processing (NLP), and multimodal interaction designs have further evolved these interfaces from functional tools into useful service providers, significantly enhancing user experience (UX) satisfaction and operational efficiency. However, in addition to the convenience, these interfaces also pose risks in terms of data security and privacy violations, making usage trust a core prerequisite for the widespread application of this technology. Future design directions must meet user needs while enhancing the transparency of the technology and data protection capabilities to explore a sustainable balance between security and intelligence. The continuous progress of AI not only increases efficiency in technological upgrades but also marks a comprehensive transformation of the industrial and social ecology. Each technological breakthrough not only breaks industry boundaries but also triggers new ethical considerations and political demands. The resolution of these multidimensional conflicts and challenges will determine the quality and scope of future AI development. How to achieve a balance between technological potential, economic interests, and social added value is crucial for promoting the role of AI in building a sustainable future.

4.1 Principles and Application Scenarios of Emotion Recognition

In the long term, the development of emotional AI describes a deeper technological ecosystem that not only performs functions at the tool level but also creates smarter and more human intelligence through understanding and reacting to emotions. This upgrade of human-machine interaction not only opens up new innovative paths in engineering and management but also promotes the in-depth integration of technology and society. Emotional AI reveals the unlimited potential of AI in our future society and opens up a vision of complete digitalization, characterized by a new level of social care.

The Rise and Potential of Emotional Artificial Intelligence

With the continuous progress in AI technology, emotion recognition technology is increasingly becoming an important pillar for further shaping human-machine interactions. This technology enables machines to understand human emotions and provides personalized and emotionally driven solutions for various fields. Through facial expressions, tone of voice, or physiological signals, emotion recognition technology is applied multidimensionally to create interactive understanding. In this section, we will delve into the mechanisms of emotion recognition and its application value in daily life and work, especially in health, education, and smart cities, as well as the central challenges and ethical dilemmas of its development.

How Emotion Recognition Technology Works

Data Collection: Multimodal Perception

Multimodal data collection forms the foundation of emotion recognition technology by capturing multiple signal sources simultaneously to analyze human emotions from various perspectives:

Speech Signal Analysis: In addition to the content of speech, features such as pitch, rhythm, and frequency range carry emotional information. For example, fast and high-frequency speech is often associated with excitement or tension, while slow and low-frequency speech may indicate fatigue or melancholy.

Facial Expression Recognition: Based on visual signals, emotions are recognized by calculating the dynamic changes in facial features (e.g., eyebrows, corners of the mouth, and eyelids). Deep learning algorithms surpass static analysis by capturing subtle changes in facial expressions through continuous video recordings.

Measurement of Physiological Signals: IoT devices and wearables (e.g., smart wristbands) can monitor skin conductivity, heart rate, breathing patterns, and brain activity to understand the biological causes of emotions. For instance, an increase in skin conductance activity is often associated with stress or fear.

By combining these data sources, emotion recognition technology can provide a precise description of users' psychological and emotional states.

Data Processing and Emotion Classification

After capturing the signals, the emotion recognition system transforms raw data into emotional outcomes through complex calculations and modeling:

Feature Extraction: Signal processing techniques extract specific emotional parameters, such as the movement of facial points in images, high-energy areas in speech spectra, or abruptly changing frequencies in heart rate curves.

Deep Learning Approaches and Emotion Modeling: Using machine learning (ML) frameworks (such as LSTM, long short-term memory), algorithmic models are created to predict emotion categories (e.g., sadness, anger, or happiness) and also capture more nuanced continuous emotion variables (such as relaxation or fatigue).

Multimodal Fusion: Individual data sources may have limitations, while the combination of speech and facial data through fusion models enables more precise identification and robustness. Multimodal systems help overcome disturbances caused by unreliable signal data.

Output and Application Design

After processing the information, emotion recognition systems output quantifiable results of users' emotional states, for example, using two-dimensional emotion coordinates "arousal" and "valence" (arousal-valence), which can be finely divided into different emotion types or probability distributions. These results serve as the basis for decision-making in various scenarios.

Typical Application Scenarios

Emotional Insights in Health Monitoring

The technology in the healthcare sector is experiencing a shift from functional to emotional adaptations. Emotion recognition not only helps increase monitoring efficiency but also becomes a tool for psychological interventions and health management.

Mental Disorder Detection: Long-term tracking of users' emotional changes enables the early identification of symptoms such as depression or anxiety. For example, a mental health app can provide personalized recommendations to users through speech or text data analysis.

Rehabilitation and Elderly Care: Emotion recognition technology in smart devices for the elderly can detect feelings of loneliness or depression, interact in a timely manner, or send alerts to family members and medical institutions.

Personalized Learning in Educational Interaction

Educational technology is changing from mere knowledge transmission to emotional support through emotion recognition, motivating students to enjoy learning more while optimizing teaching methods.

Real-time Feedback: In smart classrooms, the system analyzes students' emotions and provides teachers with direct guidance to adjust their methods. For example, if a student shows low engagement (e.g., frequently looking out the window or frowning deeply), the teacher is advised to introduce group work or dynamically change the questioning approach.

Motivation Analysis: Emotion recognition can reflect a student's current stress level based on speech tempo and behavioral patterns and adjust the course intensity accordingly to find a balance between academic challenges and mental well-being.

Improvement of Smart Cities and Public Services

The efficiency and user-friendliness of public services are significantly enhanced by emotion recognition, especially in the management of smart cities and traffic safety.

Monitoring Dangerous Driving Behavior: Using cameras or biological sensors, the psychological state of drivers is monitored in real time to reduce risks such as fatigue. For example, combining facial expression and blink frequency analysis can warn drivers with decreasing attention.

Personalized Customer Service: Online customer centers can recognize users' emotions (e.g., anger or confusion) through speech tone analysis and provide real-time suggestions on language style to improve customer satisfaction.

Technical Challenges and Ethical Issues

Technical Challenges

Despite the promising outlook for emotion recognition technology, several hurdles need to be overcome for successful implementation:

Data Quality: Signal noise and non-standardized data collection in dynamic scenarios often affect system stability. For example, background noise in speech data can interfere with emotion recognition.

Algorithm Bias and Adaptability: Training data may contain national and cultural biases, leading to insufficient recognition of emotions in certain groups. Moreover, existing models are often not optimized for scenarios involving multiple languages and cultures.

Cost and Real-Time Computation: While multimodal fusion increases precision, it complicates computations and requires significant hardware investment, which can pose a barrier to real-time application.

Ethical Issues

Emotion recognition technology delves deeply into users' privacy and behavior, necessitating the establishment of norms in the following areas:

Data Protection: Mechanisms for the collection and storage of emotional data must be transparent, and ethically contentious scenarios (e.g., covert surveillance in public spaces) must be absolutely avoided.

Emotional Manipulation Risks: The use of emotional information in commercial applications (e.g., controlling consumer behavior or imposing advertisements) can lead to trust crises and ethical controversies. In such cases, the introduction of normative restrictions is essential.

Outlook: Emotion Recognition as a Driver of Future Interactions

Emotion recognition technology is evolving into a core component of machine perception and holds immense potential for transforming healthcare, education, public services, and much more. However, for this technology to serve society rather than alienate it, technological innovation and ethical regulation must proceed hand in hand. From the optimization of multimodal approaches to privacy protection, from the development of emotion modeling to adaptation to cultural diversity, its progress depends equally on technological breakthroughs and normative measures. In the future, emotion recognition could not only redefine business models but also revolutionize the emotional connection between humans and machines.

4.2 Intelligent Customer Service: From Tools to Emotional Support

Driven by AI, intelligent customer service is evolving from mere tools for task resolution to emotionally perceptive support systems. This transformation enables machines not only to answer users' questions but also to recognize their emotional states and offer a more human-like interactive experience. The application of emotional AI is propelling this process and opening up the possibilities for intelligent, emotional customer service. This section will analyze the profound technological developments and specific application scenarios to illustrate how emotional AI is revolutionizing the customer service industry and outline the central conflicts and technical challenges of this progress.

Technological Development of Intelligent Customer Service: From Rules to Emotions

Customer service technology has significantly evolved from rule-based response systems to intelligent systems that utilize deep learning and NLP.

Rule-Based: Basic Response Logic

Traditional intelligent customer service systems rely on predefined decision trees and keyword recognition to efficiently handle structured and narrowly scoped questions, such as querying flight times or return policies. However, these rule-based "tool systems" are unable to understand complex sentence structures or ambiguous terms, let alone capture users' emotional states. This often results in interactions that feel mechanical and distant.

Enhancement of the Emotional Dimension

The introduction of emotional AI marks the key transformation from "technical problem-solving" to "emotional support" in customer service. Through technologies such as speech sentiment analysis, text emotion detection, and facial expression recognition, it is possible for intelligent systems to perceive users' emotional changes and adjust interaction strategies based on these emotions. Examples include:

If the system detects desperation in the user, it reduces the conversation speed to calm their emotions.

Emotional escalations are recognized, and the user is purposefully redirected to a human service representative.

This customer service, which enhances the emotional dimension, not only improves the UX but also establishes a positive, empathetic corporate image.

How Emotional AI Changes Customer Service Use Cases

The integration of emotional AI has added a profound emotional value to traditional customer service use cases and is driving the optimization of critical business scenarios.

Emotional Insights in Healthcare

In the healthcare sector, users are often plagued by fear, stress, or uncertainty. A virtual medical customer consultant with emotional AI can recognize users' emotions through speech variations or text inputs and offer personalized calming assistance. This assistance initially focuses on immediate emotional relief. System optimization, based on environmental factors (such as nighttime calls or critical inquiries about health issues), enables constructive communication. In the second stage, a tiered response allows users with strong emotions to be prioritized for referral to psychological support services or specialized hospital departments.

Emotional Steering of Conversations in Retail

Emotional AI can also optimize purchasing interactions in e-commerce by focusing on the psychological processes in customer buying behavior. For example, the AI can detect uncertainty, such as when a user spends a long time on a product page. In response, the system sends additional information, coupons, or user reviews to build trust. The system can also intervene in the case of negative emotions. If a user uses terms like "disappointment" or other negative words, the system adjusts the conversation to clarify misunderstandings or offer compensation to avoid cancellations.

These interactive activities based on emotion increase customer loyalty and create additional sales opportunities.

Psychological Relief in Public Services

For complex topics such as tax matters, which are often stressful for users, emotional AI can play a calming role through more human and understanding communication. Based on dynamic emotion detection, the system formulates empathetic and caring statements or strategically filtered recommendations. The system may reduce information density or simplify processes depending on the user's frustration or anger.

By optimizing communication, this application increases satisfaction with public services and reduces potential conflicts.

Resume: Contextual Understanding and User Intent Analysis

With the maturation of ML and NLP technologies, data-driven systems have emerged. This generation of customer service systems can go beyond single-point solutions by conducting semantic recognition, contextual analysis, and knowledge graph construction to engage in dynamic dialogues that meet diverse needs. However, the absence of an "emotional dimension" remains a core issue that limits UX.

4.3 Key Technological Bottlenecks and Challenges of Emotional AI

The potential of emotional AI is undoubtedly significant; however, there are key technological bottlenecks and dilemmas in comprehensive implementation and long-term development.

Dual Biases in Algorithms and Data

Emotion recognition relies on deep models and multimodal data capture, which often include biases related to gender, ethnicity, and cultural factors. Examples include:

- Cultural Differences: Some facial expressions or speech styles are interpreted differently across cultures (e.g., a smile is seen as an apology in some East Asian cultures, while it expresses warmth in Western cultures).
- Emotional Misinterpretations for Minorities: For small language communities or dialect groups, emotion recognition models may be insufficient, leading to misunderstandings or even discrimination.

Balancing Ethics and Privacy

The implementation of emotional AI heavily relies on sensitive data such as user voices, video images, or dialogue histories, which poses significant data privacy risks. Even with anonymization technologies, the possibility of data misuse remains.

Commercial Exploitation: Companies could use targeted emotional analyses to run manipulative advertising (e.g., promoting fear to sell health supplements).

Risk of Data Leaks: Customer systems that rely heavily on emotional data could become targets for cyberattacks.

Economic Barriers in Costs and Dissemination

The high technical requirements of emotional AI come with high hardware and development costs, which particularly restrict smaller companies.

Implementation Complexity: Emotional AI requires extensive and high-quality training data, which smaller companies with limited budgets find hard to provide.

Technical Hurdles: For scenarios requiring high technical maturity and language context sensitivity, current solutions are still inadequate.

Perspectives and Trends: Integration Beyond Point Applications

Emotional AI will lead intelligent customer service into an era of holistic perception and interaction across multiple scenarios. Future development possibilities include:

Intelligent Collaboration Across Platforms

With the proliferation of mobile devices, social media, and smart home technologies, the continuity of customer systems will be enhanced. For example, users can interact with an emotional customer consultant in a smart mirror in the bathroom and order product replenishments, while the system workflow seamlessly executes the order on an e-commerce platform.

Long-Term Emotion Recognition and Personalized Recommendations

Emotional AI will no longer focus solely on current emotions but will create user emotional profiles through long-term data analysis:

Historical dialogues will be used to identify emotional trends and uncover potential mental health issues.

Personal preferences from previous interactions will be taken into account to help users make decisions, such as selecting suitable products.

Global Adaptation to Culture and Language

By optimizing local semantic data and expanding culturally diverse datasets, Emotional AI will be able to achieve in-depth cultural adaptability worldwide and become a core component of international intelligent customer service systems.

Summary

Emotional AI has revitalized intelligent customer service in ways never seen before. From emotional perception to cross-platform intelligent services, this technology has completely redefined the concept of "customer service." However, technical limitations and ethical challenges remind us that a balance must be struck between technological progress and social responsibility. Collaborative efforts from interdisciplinary cooperation and policy measures will lay the foundation for the stable development of emotional AI–supported customer service.

4.4 Quality Assurance and Application Boundaries of Emotional AI

Emotional AI (also called emotion AI) endows machines with the ability to recognize and interpret nuanced human emotions, shaping the future of human-machine interaction in unprecedented ways. From health monitoring to public services, the potential of this technology is widely recognized.

The Reality and Future of Emotional Artificial Intelligence

As its applications diversify and expand, emotional AI is increasingly confronted with questions regarding technological maturity, practical performance, and ethical boundaries. Developing quality standards, accurately assessing its limitations, and identifying solutions will be crucial to promoting sustainable development in this field.

This section presents an in-depth analysis of the quality assessment criteria, current limitations, and possible solutions for the application of emotional AI from a systematic perspective, aiming to explore scientific pathways and propose practical suggestions for the future.

Core Dimensions of Quality Assessment

The effectiveness and reliability of emotional AI are highly dependent on a rigorous quality assessment system. The following core categories form the theoretical basis for evaluating the technological level and application performance:

Data Diversity and Representativeness: The breadth and quality of data form the foundation of any AI technology, and emotional AI has particularly high requirements for a diverse data base. Emotional expressions vary significantly in cultural, individual, and situational aspects. The exclusive use of data from a specific region or population group may limit the generalizability of the model and lead to misjudgments in practical applications.

Standardized Multilingual Data: Emotional AI should be trained with multilingual datasets covering various languages and dialects to enhance its global applicability.

Balanced Sampling: Data should encompass different age groups, genders, cultural backgrounds, and situational expressions to avoid biases in emotion recognition.

Multimodal Integration and Consistency: Emotional AI can improve the accuracy of emotion recognition by integrating different data sources such as speech, facial expressions, text, and body language. However, the implementation of multimodal technologies is complex as it needs to account for information conflicts, delays, and interferences. The assessment criteria are consistency and context. In terms of result consistency, the integrated analysis of multimodal data should provide coherent emotional interpretations. For contextual understanding, the systems should be able to comprehend the relationships between different modalities and enhance the accuracy of emotional prediction through contextual analysis.

UX and Adaptability: The value of emotional technologies lies not only in the precise recognition of emotions but also in their ability to understand user intentions during interactions. AI aimed at controlling emotions, improving communication quality, and building trust must be oriented toward human-centered application logic. What is important is:

Appropriate Intervention: Systems should accurately capture emotional fluctuations but avoid overinterpretation so as not to compromise the UX.

Flexible Learning System: Systems must be able to adapt their response patterns to dynamic human-machine interactions.

Data Privacy and Security: The sensitivity of emotional data demands utmost attention. Any breach in the data privacy chain, whether during data collection or usage, can lead to data misuse and harm user rights.
Important security aspects include: Multi-level approval systems for transparency in the display, management, and use of emotional data, both raw and derived data. The principle of data minimization is also crucial: Only data necessary for the specific task should be collected to avoid unnecessary storage and use.

Current Technical Limitations and Performance Deviations

Despite the deployment of emotional AI across various fields, there are pronounced discrepancies between theoretical possibilities and actual performance in practice. These issues stem from technological deficits and restricted implementation.

Data Bias and Insufficient Adaptation to Target Groups

Emotional expressions of different groups are not fully reflected in the current datasets for modeling emotional AI. Many datasets are, for instance, overly oriented toward Western cultural patterns while ignoring the subtle emotional expressions of other cultures. The reasons for this are:

The majority of emotion databases are based on a Western cultural background, making it difficult to accurately identify more nuanced emotions from other cultures (e.g., the Asian region). A smile, for example, could signify politeness rather than happiness, which can easily lead to misinterpretations by AI.

Discriminatory outcomes regarding age and gender persist as non-traditional forms of emotion are often misrecognized.

Contextual Complexity of Emotion Recognition

Emotions are not static states but are subject to the interplay of social contexts, environmental influences, and psychological conditions. Current technologies lack sufficient context analysis capabilities, which can lead to misinterpretations of complex emotional states.

Example: In a customer service scenario, a “silent pause” could signify contemplation, confusion, or even anger. Current systems often cannot suggest appropriate response strategies based on these different interpretations.

Deficiencies in Multimodal Consistency and Computational Effort

Although multimodal emotional AI has huge theoretical potential, complexity and resource consumption hinder its practical implementation. For example, when integrating video, speech, and text modalities, problems such as high computational effort and increased signal interference often arise.

Ethical Considerations and Technological Boundaries

An inescapable problem in the application of emotional AI is the ethical dilemma: Should it intrude into users' privacy or manipulate emotions through commercialization to promote, for example, consumer behavior? These questions significantly affect social acceptance.

Effective Ways to Overcome Technical and Ethical Barriers

To mitigate existing technical deficits and ethical tensions, the following strategies can contribute substantially to the future development of emotional AI:

Data Optimization for Greater Fairness and Diversity

Global Data Collaboration: Establish a global data alliance to collect representative emotional patterns, especially from minority groups, different languages, and cultures.

Dynamic Data Update Mechanism: Develop adaptive collection tools that enable continuous updating of datasets according to various application scenarios for broader coverage.

Improvement of Algorithm Transparency and Robustness

Contextual Deep Models: Integrate context-interpretation modules to support the recognition of compound emotions.

Bias-Correction Algorithms: Optimize models to reduce data bias in terms of gender, region, and cultural background.

Development of Ethical Frameworks and Legal Standards

Stakeholder Cooperation Mechanism: Collaboration between developers, companies, scientists, and policymakers to shape normative development and deployment guidelines.

Ethics Audit Tools: Introduction of independent ethics-audit models that regularly assess the alignment of AI systems with social responsibility criteria.

Promotion of Interdisciplinary Collaboration

Collaboration between different research areas is seen as a catalyst for future innovations. For example, exchanges between behavioral sciences, psychology, and social science disciplines can help avoid common errors in technology.

Important Future Prospects

Emotional AI is increasingly approaching an ideal state where human-machine interactions are characterized by empathy and understanding. However, only by resolving technical challenges and ethical conflicts can emotion AI make the transition from “emotion recognition” to “emotion understanding.” Advances in multimodal perception, context-sensitive learning, and interdisciplinary integration are expected to fundamentally change how this technology is used in service sectors, healthcare, and social governance.

Summary

Emotional AI is not only a technological but also a social revolution that requires collective contributions. Through technological rigor, ethical transparency, and enhanced social compatibility, we can look forward to a more harmonious and balanced relationship between humans and technology in an intelligent future.

4.5 Emotion Data for Optimizing User Experience (UX)

In the age of digital progress and the rapid development of AI, the focus of UX design is increasingly shifting from a functional to an emotional perspective. While traditional UX optimization is based on logical problem-solving and process improvements, leveraging emotions as a driving force of data enables a deeper understanding of users’ psychological needs and emotional states. Supported by advancements in AI, emotion data allows for the recognition and response to feelings, thereby creating unique interactions that fundamentally redefine the value of UXs.

This section explores the theoretical foundations and practical role of emotions as a driving force of data. It also analyzes application pathways, technological prerequisites, and challenges in implementation. The goal is to highlight practical innovation solutions for businesses and developers.

Theoretical Framework of Emotion-Driven Data

As an emerging research field, emotion-driven data utilization encompasses a variety of interrelated concepts and technical dimensions. This driving force combines emotion recognition technologies, behavioral data analysis, and real-time interaction models to transition UXs from static to dynamic improvement cycles.

The core theoretical foundations include:

Affective Computing: The recognition of facial expressions, vocal intonations, and physiological signals creates a cycle of emotion detection and response.

Cognitive Load Models: These models reduce users' mental effort by integrating emotional data, thereby optimizing interaction efficiency.

Experience Economy: Against the backdrop of the experience economy, emotional drive is seen as the key to satisfying users' deeper needs.

Dynamic Adaptation Theory: By real-time recognition of emotional states, interaction strategies can be continuously adjusted to achieve sustainable optimization of UX.

Application Pathways: From Data Collection to Experience Loop

The practical use of emotion-driven data covers the entire cycle from data collection to experience design and integrates several key technologies.

Emotion Data Collection

The primary sources of emotion data are perception-based data (e.g., facial expressions and vocal intonations) and physiological data (e.g., pulse, breathing rate). The accuracy of emotion analysis is significantly enhanced through the use of deep learning and multimodal integration.

Example: In retail, cameras analyze facial expressions to determine customer satisfaction and adjust product recommendations accordingly.

Development of Emotion Models

After data collection, emotion models are developed to differentiate emotional states. High-quality models need to balance generalizability, adaptability, and cultural sensitivity.

Technological focus: Increasing sensitivity to subtle emotional differences, such as distinguishing between "anxiety" and "sadness" in different contexts.

Emotional Control and Response Optimization

The results of emotion models significantly influence the design of user interactions. Adjusting content, vocal intonations, or interface components based on users' emotions is a core method for implementing emotion-driven approaches.

Data Loop and Continuous Optimization

User feedback is collected as feedback data to improve models. Positive reactions to specific design approaches enhance the models' ability to adapt to similar situations.

Technological Support: Case Analysis

Case 1: Emotionally Driven Systems in Customer Service

In the realm of customer service, the integration of emotional data can help simulate empathy, thereby increasing user satisfaction.

Technological Process:

Emotion Detection from Speech: Analyzing tone and vocal patterns to detect emotions such as joy, fear, anger, or disappointment.

Adaptation of Interaction Methods: Modulating response strategies in accordance with emotional states to reduce tension.

Real-Time Solutions: Predefined problem-solving pathways for negative emotions to reduce wait times.

Results: A major telecommunications provider was able to increase customer satisfaction by 25% and reduce repeat complaint rates by nearly 20% through emotional steering.

Case 2: Emotional Health Management Platforms

In the area of mental well-being, the use of emotional data shows tremendous potential. A technological highlight in this area is the integration of physiological data. Wearables capture data for heart rate, blood pressure, oxygen saturation, etc., and these data are combined with speech analysis to assess emotional states. Based on this, personalized feedback can be given, for example, in the form of individually created plans for meditation or exercise. User feedback showed that an emotional support app was able to effectively help 58% of users reduce stress and anxiety.

Core Conflicts and Technological Limitations

Despite the promise of emotionally driven interactions, there are numerous challenges regarding technology and application:

Technological Complexity and Costs

The integration of multimodal data requires substantial computational resources, and the high costs of hardware pose additional difficulties. Smaller companies have trouble deploying such technologies on a large scale.

Data Biases and Lack of Robustness

Misclassifications due to model deviations, for example among older people or minorities, negatively impact the UX.

Transparency and Explainability of Algorithms

Many emotional recognition systems are a "black box," which could affect users' trust in the technology.

Cultural Differences and Lack of Adaptation

The interpretation of emotions varies significantly across cultures. A global model often encounters limitations, such as the low intensity of emotional expression by East Asian users, which is often misinterpreted as "emotionlessness."

Data Privacy and Ethical Risks

Since emotional data is extremely sensitive, misuse, such as manipulation for targeted advertising, could bring serious social problems.

Practical Recommendations for Implementation

To expand the application possibilities of emotional data, the following measures are recommended:

Promotion of Multimodal Technology Integration: Developing efficient algorithms and promoting open standards to lower barriers to entry for developers.

Building Culturally Sensitive Models: Interdisciplinary collaboration among experts in cultural studies, psychology, and technology to optimize models.

Strengthening Data Privacy: End-to-end encryption and transparent guidelines for data usage to bolster user trust.

Promoting Transparency and User Education: Developing explainable algorithms and providing easily understandable educational resources to foster technology acceptance.

Cross-Industry Collaboration and Political Support: Promoting synergistic research between data science, psychology, and sociology, as well as establishing global ethical standards.

Market Perspectives and Outlook

Emotion-driven data is increasingly becoming the core of future human-machine interactions. It is being expanded from specialized areas to more industries and use cases. With decreasing investment costs for hardware and software, growing transparency, and well-considered ethical standards, this technology will revolutionize the understanding of user relationships and elevate services and product offerings to a new level of UX.

The use of emotions has not only a technological but also a psychological dimension. It encourages us to move from functional designs to emotional connections and opens a more human-centered perspective for shaping the future of everyday life and work.

4.6 The Development and Application of Intelligent Assistants

Intelligent interaction interfaces are revolutionizing the way information is presented and the way human-machine interaction is designed. At the core is the deep integration of AI with emotions, which enables a natural and fluid UX. In recent years, the development of interfaces has evolved from simple key-based operations to voice, touch, visual, and multimodal interaction systems. This not only increases user friendliness but also adds an emotional dimension to the interaction, where interfaces are evolving from mechanical tools to intelligent assistants. This shift promotes the restructuring of workflows and the innovation of service models in areas such as education, healthcare, and retail.

Speech recognition and NLP are central drivers of this interface revolution. Their expansion into smart devices and diverse application scenarios demonstrates the benefits of combining language understanding and emotional perception. From the development of ChatGPT to intelligent voice assistants, capabilities for dialogue generation and user context recognition have made great progress, making interactions more precise and emotional. This not only changes the UX but also fundamental functions such as personalized decision-making support and user companionship. These developments profoundly influence consumer habits and users' technological dependence.

With facial expression recognition, gesture control, and multimodal interaction technology, users can overcome the limitations of traditional interfaces and interact more naturally. Examples include applications for monitoring facial expressions in elderly care or gesture control in special education, which highlight the potential advantages of such technologies in terms of fairness and inclusive design. Multimodal interactions that integrate voice, sight, and touch overcome the limitations of individual modes and offer solutions for the needs of diverse and complex scenarios.

The rapid development of intelligent interaction interfaces brings numerous technical and ethical challenges. Particularly noteworthy are data privacy and data security issues once again. Interaction systems must process a large amount of behavioral and emotional data to optimize their models. These data are often at risk of misuse or leaks. The lack of transparent and trustworthy usage regulations could reinforce algorithmic biases or shake users' trust. Another challenge is to balance universality and cultural adaptability. Some designs that are too specialized may not work in different regions or population groups, which require a balance and breakthrough through extensive user feedback.

In the future, intelligent interaction interfaces will continue to develop toward deeper UXs and technological extensions and will establish themselves as core components of productivity tools and service systems. Advances in semantic understanding and emotional feedback from household assistants or the integration of multimodal interfaces to optimize multitasking processes in industry show the potential for a higher level of interaction. However, the coordination between technological development and social responsibility requires a reasonable balance between the speed of innovation and the ethical framework. This process not only demands interdisciplinary collaboration in advanced technologies but also a firm commitment to user-centered design to promote and implement a smarter and more sustainable way of interaction in the information age.

The Development of Intelligent Assistants

The emergence of intelligent assistants can be traced back to the 1990s when rule-based systems first took shape. These early systems, such as Microsoft's Clippy or simple research assistants, employed pre-defined conditions to perform specific actions. However, they lacked flexibility and the ability to understand context. They were heavily restricted to performing simple tasks, which initially prevented them from being integrated into complex scenarios.

In the twenty-first century, advancements in NLP, speech recognition, and ML led to the development of data-driven systems. Representatives of this stage of development are Apple's Siri, Amazon's Alexa, and the Google Assistant. These assistants are based on deep learning technologies and can understand and respond to natural language commands in real time. They enable complex activities such as navigation, music playback, or control of smart-home devices. This phase was characterized by a transition from simple tools to platforms that enable semantic processing.

Recently, intelligent assistants have entered a new era with the advent of generative AI, as seen in ChatGPT. These tools utilize large-scale language models and demonstrate the ability to generate natural, context-related, and emotional interactions. Supported by multimodal interaction designs (voice, visual, and haptic elements), intelligent assistants have transcended their role as mere command receivers. They have become deeply embedded partners in users' daily lives, professional settings, and industrial applications and collaborations. Thus, they have evolved from "task-centered tools" to "knowledge-centered companions," emphasizing their universal applicability across various fields.

Cross-Industry Application of Intelligent Assistants

The technological progress of intelligent assistants not only drives the improvement of UX but also profoundly changes the production and service models of many industries. The following highlights some key areas and their specific application scenarios as well as the added value.

Healthcare

In healthcare, intelligent assistants open up new possibilities in patient care and information management, especially in telemedicine and diagnostic support. For example, systems driven by speech processing can allow patients to describe their symptoms and provide initial recommendations, thereby significantly improving the efficiency of healthcare resources. These assistants also show great potential in linking medical data. They can offer personalized advice on exercise or nutrition, especially in the management of chronic diseases.

Moreover, these assistants can provide doctors with solid decision-making foundations by efficiently analyzing medical literature. For example, some assistants can also address specific clinical requirements, extract relevant documents, and provide information on treatment methods and medications. However, data privacy remains a huge challenge in the application of such systems. Balancing the use of data with the protection of patients' rights remains a central topic in the discussion of ethical and technological responsibility.

Education

In the education sector, intelligent assistants are widely used to support learning processes and personalized learning. Learning assistants based on voice-based dialogue systems can not only directly respond to students' questions but also analyze individual learning progress and recommend corresponding content. This personalized approach is particularly suitable for self-directed learning environments, significantly increasing learning efficiency.

In the classroom, intelligent assistants optimize the teaching environment with functions such as voice control and augmented reality. Teachers can present course materials with interactive whiteboards or capture notes in real time, so they can focus on their pedagogical tasks. Moreover, by analyzing students' behavior, problem areas can be identified, promoting the shift from experience-based to data-driven teaching.

Financial Services and Business Management

In the financial sector, intelligent assistants have gained importance as tools for efficiency optimization. Banks, for example, use them to support customer services, where they handle inquiries about account balances, transaction histories, or loan options around the clock. These automated services, often based on deep ML, reduce costs while increasing customer satisfaction.

In business management, intelligent assistants are increasingly taking on key roles in optimizing business processes. For example, they can analyze historical data as budget management systems to predict future financial trends. In the supply chain, similar assistants can ensure precise coordination and management of resources by analyzing current data. These systems have proven indispensable in practice for increasing efficiency and making well-informed business decisions.

Summary and Prospects

Intelligent interaction interfaces are transforming human-machine communication by integrating AI with emotional intelligence. Their evolution has moved from basic key-based controls to advanced voice, touch, visual, and multimodal systems, offering a more natural and engaging UX. Speech recognition and NLP technologies are central, enhancing personalization and emotional connection in digital interactions. These advancements have changed user behavior, increasing both technological reliance and the scope of personalized decision support. Technology such as facial expression recognition and gesture control improves accessibility and inclusivity, especially in sectors like elder care and special education. However, collecting and processing vast amounts of behavioral and emotional data raises significant concerns about data privacy and security. The future will see intelligent interfaces becoming core productivity and service tools, with ongoing improvements in semantic understanding and emotional feedback. Historically, intelligent assistants have evolved from rigid, rule-based systems to highly adaptive, context-aware platforms. The current generation, powered by generative AI and multimodal design, serves as knowledge-centered companions across industries. Ultimately, these developments demand a balance between technological innovation and ethical responsibility to ensure sustainable progress.

Chapter 5
Generative AI in Content Creation and Cultural Dissemination

Generative artificial intelligence (AI) is increasingly becoming a key driver of digital transformation in many industries, and its technological advancements show profound potential for change in the fields of cultural and creative industries, industrial production, and commercial services. In the creative industry, generative AI, with its ability to quickly create content in various formats and high quality, significantly increases the efficiency of creatives and inspires innovative forms of artistic expression. For example, its experimental applications in visual arts and text generation have transcended the traditional boundaries of creation and intensified the interaction between works and the audience. However, this technology raises urgent questions about the protection of intellectual property and the definition of originality, highlighting the need for a solid legal basis to properly safeguard the rights of creatives.

In the industrial sector, the influence of generative AI is particularly pronounced, especially in the optimization of production processes and model development. From the development of automated devices to the optimization of solution proposals, generative AI significantly increases manufacturing efficiency through the simulation of multi-variable scenarios and dynamic analyses, helping companies quickly adapt to dynamic market demands. In addition, its application in supply chain management improves flexibility in resource allocation and planning, offering companies greater operational agility. However, technical limitations such as the lack of adaptability of models and the reliability of generated results pose challenges in the practical implementation of generative AI. Therefore, continuous progress is needed in both algorithm optimization and the design of application scenarios.

The economic value of generative AI is not only reflected in increased operational efficiency but also creates new ways for companies to reshape business models. For example, its use in personalized content creation and product design shows huge market potential by creating highly individualized consumer experiences through in-depth analysis and rapid response to customer needs. In areas such as education, entertainment, and e-commerce, generative AI is used to increase the interactivity of business processes and strengthen customer loyalty, thereby promoting closer connections between brands and consumers. However, this technology also raises further questions about data privacy. Companies must ensure transparent and lawful processing of user data and maintain a balance between technological innovation and ethical standards.

Numerous success stories confirm the broad applicability of generative AI in business practice, such as in optimizing scenes in film production, animation generation,

 | https://doi.org/10.1515/9783112242728-005

and automated text creation in the advertising industry. These examples illustrate the potential of the technology to significantly reduce costs and increase the efficiency of creative processes. At the same time, they point to limitations in the quality and diversity of generated content, prompting research institutions and companies to advance the development of more inclusive model architectures and innovative designs.

Whether generative AI will become a cross-industry engine of change depends ultimately on the balance between technological progress and social responsibility. Only through rigorous technological advancement combined with the creation of transparent regulations and social regulatory mechanisms can the potential of generative AI be fully realized and a sustainable innovation ecosystem be promoted.

The rapid technological advancements of generative AI are profoundly influencing production methods, business processes, and societal perceptions in the field of cultural creativity and dissemination. Its ability for deep learning and data generation is changing the boundaries of content creation while simultaneously sparking a complex discussion about copyright protection, ethical standards, and the rights of creatives. The question of how to achieve a balanced equilibrium between technological benefits and cultural value has become a central concern for both society and industry.

Generative AI demonstrates a new form of creativity in content production and industrial design that goes beyond traditional tools through its applications. It is capable of automatically generating a variety of outcomes, such as texts, images, and even complex design models. This not only provides new approaches for cultural dissemination and digital media but also opens up new possibilities for business model innovation. However, this immense creative power comes with controversies regarding originality and copyright, especially when verifying the authorship of generated content. The industry must develop universal standards and intelligent control mechanisms to promote a balanced relationship between technological value and ethical requirements. In addition, the further development of intelligent interaction technologies is fundamentally changing the principles of information dissemination and access.

5.1 Technological Evolution and the Innovative Role of Generative AI

Generative AI utilizes deep learning and generative adversarial networks to transform large amounts of data into versatile and intelligent content. This not only increases the efficiency of creation but also expands the expressive possibilities for creatives. Each step of its creative logic implies a fundamental transformation of the industry, from craft-based production to intelligent control.

Breakthroughs in Text Generation and Semantic Optimization

The remarkable capabilities of generative AI in text creation are evident both in the precise and appealing generation of content based on semantic analysis and in the optimization of personalization and scalability of communication content. For example, the GPT series from OpenAI has established itself as an important tool in the fields of advertising copywriting, e-commerce text design, and news writing. Using large amounts of data, these models not only optimize speech acts but also enhance the efficiency of communication strategies through situational language understanding.

A significant application example is an international e-commerce platform that uses GPT technology to create personalized recommendations for advertising copy. This intelligent generation tool increased the open rate of e-mails by 32% and improved the quality of consumer interaction. Such applications confirm the economic benefits and business value of generative AI in increasing the efficiency of the content-creation process.

Immediate Advantages in Design and Image Generation

In the realm of visual content, generative AI enables the creation of images through the analysis of keywords, sketches, and themes, becoming an indispensable technological support for advertising, brand communication, and social media operations. This capability not only reduces dependence on professional design skills but also offers new pathways for small businesses or independent creatives with limited resources. For instance, DALL-E technology (a computer program developed by OpenAI that translates text prompts into images) combines natural language processing with visual presentation to generate precise and personalized images based on complex textual descriptions.

A particularly in-depth application scenario is an international educational platform that utilizes generative AI technology to create teaching posters and supporting illustrations. By contextualizing and situating visual content, the learning experience of students has been optimized, and the form of cultural dissemination has been expanded. The rapid adaptation and dissemination of content directly contribute to the equalization of global educational resources.

Dynamic Video Generation and Expanded Collaboration in Film Production

The role of generative AI in the video domain is particularly prominent, including automated editing, scene editing, and optimization of computer-generated imagery effects. For example, the Runway ML platform offers automated functions for creating video clips, reducing editing time and enhancing flexibility in post-production.

A case from the film industry: A Hollywood special effects company uses generative AI to automatically create complex scene models and renderings. This increased the efficiency of special effects production by about 40% and significantly reduced production costs. This not only illustrates the value that AI adds to traditional content production but also paves the way for applications in other industries.

Innovative Potential and Impact of AI on Cultural Dissemination

The integration of generative AI has not only changed production methods but also enhanced imagination and expanded the globalization potential of cultural dissemination. Its positive impact on cultural diversity, interactivity, and inclusion demonstrates the great potential for a technological and cultural symbiosis.

Diversity and Depth in Cross-Cultural Content Creation

Generative AI excels at integrating a variety of cultural elements. By analyzing linguistic characteristics and artistic expressions from different regions worldwide, it enables a differentiated approach to the dissemination of cultural content. For example, it automatically generates localized movie subtitles or song lyrics, accelerating content localization and increasing the speed of dissemination.

A prominent example is an international fashion company that uses generative AI to publish globally adapted advertising copy. Successfully achieving cultural resonance with consumers in various regions, the advertisement's click-through rate was increased by a total of 50%. This capability for efficient content creation not only helps companies achieve outstanding performance in target markets but also creates more contextual space for global cultural content.

Innovative Models of Personalized Dissemination and Creative User Participation

Generative AI breaks the traditional “one-way creation model” and opens up new mechanisms for user participation. For example, a novel-generating platform allows users to make creative suggestions, based on which AI generates actions and texts. This enhanced participation brings creative people and audiences closer together and unleashes the latent creativity of society.

This content creation ecosystem not only changes the traditional structure centered on the author but also gradually forms an innovative user-based content creation business model. This not only promotes consumer experience but also gives rise to vibrant cultural expressions.

Contradictions and Ethics: Focus Issues in the Transformation Process

The rapid development of generative AI also brings key conflicts, including copyright protection, ethical guidelines, and the distribution of profits between humans and technology. A clear institutional framework is crucial to ensuring the healthy development of the cultural industry.

Legal Vacuum in the Attribution of Intellectual Property

Currently, the ownership of works created by generative AI is open to heated debate from legal and ethical perspectives. It is unclear whether it belongs to the developer, the model provider, or the end-user. For example, in terms of original innovations such as new-type visual posters or literary texts, the question arises as to how responsibilities and ownership can be fairly distributed. Without clear answers, the industrialization of technological innovation may be hindered.

Challenges to Credibility from False Content

Uncontrolled generative AI may produce misleading or false content, as is the case with deepfake technology, which has been misused for political purposes or online fraud. These issues not only threaten the credibility of cultural dissemination but also affect the trustworthiness of technology and information in society. Society rightly demands clear regulations and prohibitions.

Future Outlook on Balancing Human and AI Rights

The further development of generative technologies may put economic pressure on traditional creatives, especially in terms of copyright competition and displacement processes. Possible solutions may include a labeling obligation for AI-generated content and legal protection measures for creatives.

Shared Vision for Technological and Cultural Development

Generative AI is not only used for content creation but also promotes collaboration with human creatives to enhance the overall efficiency of the cultural industry. This creates new opportunities for technology-assisted cultural dissemination, while governments, businesses, and developers are called upon to create fairer legal frameworks and standards.

Future trends may include a deeper integration of technology and art, the widespread application of collaborative content platforms, and strengthened cross-cultural cooperation. This will not only inject unprecedented vitality into global cultural dissemination but also promote a balance between technological development and social value, creating a richer and more diverse cultural landscape for the benefit of society.

Conclusion

The immense power of generative AI is driving the transformation of content creation, cultural dissemination, and user interaction. However, its promotion requires the application of ethical and regulatory principles to ensure that innovations serve the long-term interests of society. With well-considered rules and collective support, generative AI could become an indispensable engine for creativity and cultural development, while ushering in a new era of collaboration between humans and technology.

5.2 The Technological Intersection of Entertainment and Industry

Both in entertainment and industry, the cross-domain capability of generative AI shapes new forms of collaborative innovation. For example, the visual simulation competence from the construction industry can be applied in both the film and engineering sectors. Meanwhile, the film industry's experience in processing large-scale real-time rendering data serves as a reference for the manufacturing industry, such as in the distribution of computing resources in multi-process scenarios.

Sustainable Design and Bidirectional Learning

The experience of industrial intelligence feeds back into the entertainment industry, leading to more sustainable resource utilization and lower costs. For example, the application of dynamic modeling of sustainable production lines essentially also allows for a significant reduction in resource consumption in the production of feature films. In addition, the film production industry is already using intelligent algorithms developed by the industry to optimize shooting schedules and minimize the risk of costly reshoots.

A Glimpse into the Future: The Boundless Expansion of Generative AI

A Smart Roadmap Through Interdisciplinary Collaboration

At the intersection of entertainment and industry, the potential of generative AI unfolds further through interdisciplinary collaboration. In medical image analysis, more effective diagnostic tools are developed; in agriculture, generative modeling helps optimize planting patterns and withstand extreme climate conditions. Combined with the social sciences, cultural simulation systems that predict political decisions and their social impacts could even emerge.

The Long-Term Question of Ethics and Regulation

As this technology continues to spread, society is no longer faced with the question of whether to apply generative AI, but how. In the future, the development of more empathetic algorithms may equip generative AI with more “emotional intelligence” and enrich cultural expressions. At the same time, a security-oriented and strict responsibility framework in the industry will be essential to build a smart and equal society.

Generative AI breaks traditional boundaries and creates a long-term technological foundation that serves both efficiency and creativity. Only by balancing the potential and ethical challenges of application can this technology truly make its optimal contribution to the sustainable development of society.

The Impact from Entertainment to Industry

The rise of generative AI means that humanity is no longer reliant solely on linear innovation but has made a leap into an algorithm-driven, omnipresent change. From unleashing creative achievements in the cultural sphere to the efficiency revolution in industry, generative modeling technology is driving the transformation of industry ecosystems.

The Dual Engine of Technological Change

This technological capability is not limited to the generation of images, audio, and texts but also optimizes and reorganizes complex systems. The broad penetration of different fields makes generative AI a dual engine that combines creativity and efficiency.

Application of Generative Modeling in Culture and Entertainment

Content Creation: Redefining Creative Logic

The growth curve of generative AI in the field of culture and entertainment shows that it is no longer just a tool but is redefining the paradigms of creativity. Whether in literature, film, or art, the presence of AI allows creatives to overcome the "downtime" of inspiration. Large-scale language models (such as GPT) can enable rapid generation of plot frameworks based on keywords and provide a variety of impulses for literary creation. On the visual level, tools like DALL-E and MidJourney use huge image databases to generate impressive design concepts and significantly simplify the conceptualization process in the art field.

A real-life example shows an independent animation studio using generative AI for the design of characters and scenes. Combined with traditional 3D-modelling tools, the project timeline was shortened by 32% and the output quality was significantly improved. From an efficiency perspective, generative technology not only closes the gaps in human creative inefficiency but also restructures the creative process and team collaboration.

Music and Interactive Entertainment: Industrial Breakthroughs

In the field of music production, generative AI, with its multifunctional and context-sensitive properties, is already being extensively used. Platforms such as MuseNet and AIVA can generate accurate melodies and harmonies based on emotional, stylistic, and historical parameters. An independent musician used AI to create the basic melody of a concept EP (Extended Play) and only needed two days to complete the work, a time saving of 70% compared to traditional processes.

Interactive entertainment is another field where generative AI can play to its strengths. With the rise of open-world and immersive games, the logic of generated non-player characters and multi-layered environmental designs have become key challenges for the industry. Generative technologies refine scene dynamics and character behavior patterns, contributing to a more realistic gaming experience. For example, the game "Cyberpunk 2077" experimentally implemented generative algorithms to dynamically shape social ecosystems in an urban environment, significantly improving the gaming experience.

Challenges: Copyright and Risks of Homogenization

Despite the advantages of generative AI, it also brings potential dangers for copyright protection and creative diversity. Since generations are based on existing databases, conflicts may arise within the current legal framework of intellectual property. In addition, there is the risk that mass-produced content could lead to cultural homogenization and irreparably deplete the creative landscape. Solutions include the development of specific rules for copyright distribution, the protection of individual data sources, and the collaboration of public and commercial data resources.

Model Generation in Industry: Efficiency Revolution and Accelerated Results

Intelligent Design Leaps in Industrial Design

Generative AI has ushered in a new era of automated design in industry. Whether it is the intelligent modeling of product components or the optimization of machine structures, the modeling capabilities of AI penetrate the core of traditional industrial design. For example, in the experimental projects of aircraft manufacturers, generative algorithms accelerated the structural iteration of aircraft parts, enabling a 10% reduction in materials and an increase in production precision. In the construction industry, AI-based models have introduced new methods for modular construction, with optimized building plans being automatically generated and a significant reduction in resource waste.

More importantly, generative technologies are capable of dynamically adjusting design plans based on operational data, creating an integrated optimization process from concept development to the entire lifecycle management. For example, in automated production lines in manufacturing, the generative model can generate alternative designs to immediately fix component failures, significantly reducing downtime.

Real-time Optimization and Simulation of Production Processes

Generative AI not only improves core design but also increases the precision and flexibility of production processes. In manufacturing plants, hundreds of layout options are simulated with generative AI to significantly increase production efficiency at fixed costs. Similarly, generative modeling is used to optimize raw material resources: a multinational corporation was able to reduce global supply chain risks by 40% during the pandemic using data-driven models.

Virtual production processes are now becoming a leading approach for industrial transformation. With generative modeling, digital twins can offer dynamic simulations of a variety of processes and test the effects of different strategies. For example, a semiconductor company was able to optimize power consumption and increase the stability of its production lines by using a virtual factory environment, a typical example of generative AI as a boost to industrial management capabilities.

Ethical Challenges in Corporate Structural Changes

The advantages of generative AI in industry also bring social concerns about possible "technological derailment." For example, complete dependence on AI analysis and model creation could lead to job cuts and increased dependence on technology. In addition, the use of internal corporate data for model training should be regulated with clearly defined boundaries of responsibility to avoid unfair "Algorithmic exploitation."

5.3 Creativity and Copyright: How to Balance Technology and Ethics

Generative AI is rapidly changing the boundaries of the creative industry and industrial production by generating text, music, images, and optimized design solutions with unprecedented efficiency and scalability. This revolutionary technology not only redefines productivity but also highlights complex contradictions in the field of originality and copyright protection.

Challenges of the New Era of Generative AI

The overall question is: Who owns the copyright to AI-generated content? How is the originality of machine-generated content defined? These questions not only challenge existing legal frameworks but also raise ethical and social conflicts.

This section examines the impact of generative AI on copyright protection and ethical standards, from the technical basis to legal challenges, from social impacts to suggested solutions. The goal is to point out ways to coordinate technology, culture, and rules.

Impact of Generative AI on Traditional Copyright Systems

Ownership: Legal Anchoring and Grey Areas

Currently, the rights to generative AI works are a legal field without clear global guidelines. Traditional copyright is based on the principle of "human creation," but AI-generated content is not directly created by humans but through complex algorithmic calculations. The question arises: If a user generates a piece of art or an article through an AI model, does the content belong to the user, the technology provider, the developer of the trained AI model, or should there be a new category of "non-human author"? The legal uncertainty creates uncertainty in the practice of the creative economy.

Datasets and Originality: Reshaping Copyright

Generative AI often relies on extensive datasets that are publicly available or provided through licensing agreements but often contain copyrighted material. Is this considered "passive reference"? Can generated content be seen as independent original works? Often, AI-generated content shows traces of the training data, thereby raising questions about the infringement of the rights of the original authors. For example, an AI-generated painting that closely resembles the style of a well-known artist could be seen as an algorithmic imitation or a new form of creative expression. The vague standards for originality call for a redefinition of copyright.

Copyright Inflation and Market Imbalance

The ability of generative AI to produce content in large quantities greatly increases production speed and volume but also brings the risk of "copyright inflation." Large amounts of low-quality or repetitive content flood the market, which may reduce the market value of human creations, shorten the life cycle of content, and endanger the differentiation and uniqueness of cultural creations. This is not only a challenge for the creative economy but also for maintaining cultural diversity in society.

Ethical Debates: Cultural and Social Challenges in Technological Progress

Data Misuse and Privacy Violations

AI's training data mostly comes from publicly available internet sources that may not be authorized or contain sensitive private information. If this data is used for commercial content without the consent of the authors, the question arises as to whether rights are being violated. Establishing standardized legal procedures to ensure data legitimacy is not only an ethical necessity but also a key step for the further development of the industry.

Displacement of Creative Workforce

The progressive integration of generative AI in literature, advertising, design, and other fields puts pressure on traditional creative professions. For example, the rapid generation of advertising copy may reduce the demand for professional copywriters, and in the design field, AI is increasingly replacing the role of junior designers. If this trend continues, it may lead to an imbalance in the labor market, marginalize creative professionals, and ultimately contribute to social inequality.

Technological Bias and the Risk of Homogeneous Culture

AI models learn from existing datasets, which often contain cultural, gender-specific, or regional biases. In addition, generated content tends to cater to the mainstream, which can weaken uniqueness and avant-garde. This may not only reinforce existing social biases but also undermine the innovation power of the cultural industry in the long run.

5.4 A Harmonious Development Plan for Technology and Society

The future copyright system must take into account the particularities of generative AI and develop dynamic standards for rights implementation. For example, a model based on "dual-level rights" could be considered: contributions from users and technology developers could be clearly separated by distinguishing the algorithmic part of content creation from human input. Such a demarcation would enable a fair distribution of earnings and honor both technological and human creativity.

Introduction of Transparent Mechanisms and Open Platforms

Explainability technologies in machine learning and blockchain technologies could be employed to trace the origin of content and define copyright boundaries. For instance, implementing traceability levels by embedding digital watermarks in generated content or encrypting training data could efficiently resolve disputes.

Profit Sharing and Open Collaboration Platforms

A data sharing and profit participation mechanism could be created to use copyrighted material under fair-use principles. For example, AI companies could enter into licensing agreements with copyright holders to ensure a fair distribution of revenues. Such a solution would not only promote social justice but also boost knowledge sharing.

Development of Ethical Standards for the Industry

Ethical guidelines should be seen as a complement to legal frameworks. Establishing uniform industry standards is a crucial step. Ethical guidelines could include mechanisms for bias correction, rules for diversity preservation, and transparency in data usage. These standards would increase societal acceptance of generative AI and create valuable practical experiences for future laws.

Interdisciplinary and Cross-Industry Collaboration

The challenges posed by generative AI cannot be tackled by legal and technological solutions alone. It is equally important to involve ethicists, economists, and cultural scientists. By setting up cross-technology platforms and collaborative organizations that pool knowledge from various disciplines, the sustainable development of generative AI could be ensured, and thus a balance between technology and culture could be maintained.

Examples: From Conflict to Solution-oriented Practice

Example 1: Implementation of Profit Sharing in Music Copyright

A melody generated by AI closely resembled the work of a well-known musician. Through a profit sharing agreement and transparent tracking mechanisms, the conflict was successfully resolved. This example shows how musicians' rights could be protected while also establishing fair treatment of AI-inspired works, as a possible blueprint for the industry.

Example 2: Collaboration for Transparent Datasets

A fashion company and a technology provider jointly developed an AI-design tool that exclusively used licensed and authorized training material. This kind of cross-industry collaboration sets standards for the lawful use of training data and ensures that data privacy and ethical responsibility are maintained.

Future Outlook: An Ecosystem in Dynamic Equilibrium

Generative AI represents not only a technological breakthrough but also a reshaping of societal rules. Developers, legal experts, and the creative industry must collaborate in open dialogue to achieve a balance between innovation and protection.

Copyright and ethical standards must remain integral parts of the development of generative AI. On this basis, with intelligent solutions and fair agreements, an environment that reconciles innovation, justice, and progress can be created. These approaches will not only shape the future direction of technology but also the sustainable development of culture and society as a whole.

5.5 Potentials and Barriers of Generative AI in Corporate Innovation

In a fast-paced economy, generative AI shows a rapidly growing potential for innovation. This groundbreaking technology offers companies comprehensive support, ranging from content creation to process optimization.

The Rise of Generative AI and the Transformation of Corporate Innovation

However, its impressive capabilities come with uncertainties, application barriers, and ethical challenges. How companies can successfully implement and scale generative AI is an urgent topic that involves both opportunities and challenges.

Main Application Scenarios of Generative AI in Companies

Intelligent Content Production and Creative Innovation

Generative AI can produce high-quality content quickly and efficiently, especially in content-driven industries such as advertising, public relations, and media. Text-based generative AI models (such as ChatGPT or Claude) enable companies to automatically create advertising copy, customer information, or even entire articles. Image-generating models (such as DALL-E and MidJourney) are also revolutionizing visual design and marketing.

This not only shortens production times but also increases personalization possibilities and targeting in content distribution. Compared to traditional manual creation, generative AI offers a scalable approach to content production.

Example: An e-commerce platform uses generative AI to create personalized advertising copy on a large scale based on user behavior data. With automatically designed advertising images in different styles, the buyer share in campaigns was increased by 22% compared to traditional methods.

Industrial Design and Accelerated Product Innovation

Generative AI shows exceptional creativity in overcoming previous limitations in industrial design. In product development, AI can not only generate multiple design concepts but also identify market trends and predict the popularity of certain designs through algorithmic analysis. In engineering, AI supports the optimization of manufacturing processes, material selection, component design, and production workflows, significantly increasing production efficiency.

Additionally, generative AI helps shorten the development time for prototypes by using virtual models for testing to validate creative ideas early on.

Example: An aerospace company used generative AI to analyze aerodynamic simulations and reduced the development time for prototype designs from 18 months to 9 months.

Intelligent Optimization of Business Processes

Generative AI is increasingly being integrated into the management of operational business processes. It enables automation in personnel selection and performance evaluation, supports market analysis, and optimizes supply chains. By integrating historical sales data and market trends, language models can not only write market reports but also create clear strategic action plans.

In the supply chain, AI generates dynamic optimization scenarios, predicts purchasing and logistics needs, minimizes cost waste, and increases flexibility in operational execution. These innovations make traditional processes more efficient and agile in the face of rapidly changing market demands.

Example: A global trading company used generative AI to analyze customer purchasing habits to develop customized offer campaigns and simultaneously reduced excess inventory by 15% through improved demand forecasting.

Practical Barriers and Potential Risks in Application

Data Quality and Fairness Issues

The capabilities of generative AI depend on high-quality datasets, but corporate-owned data is often fragmented, incomplete, or biased. This reduces the accuracy of model predictions and can inadvertently amplify the biases contained in the data. For example, a model that misinterprets regional consumption habits could generate flawed product strategies and advertising plans.

Warning Example: A fashion brand used generative AI to create personalized consumer recommendations but ignored the overrepresentation of urban consumption cultures in the training dataset, leading to a misjudgment of the rural market.

Robustness and Adaptability of Technology

When implementing generative AI, model stability and adaptability pose particular challenges. Many pre-trained models perform excellently in controlled environments but encounter limitations in specific, rapidly changing industry scenarios. Content generated by generative AI may not reflect brand identity or may even damage a company's reputation.

Example: An international consumer goods brand used generative AI to create multilingual advertising copy. However, the model failed to understand cultural nuances, resulting in an advertising copy with offensive content and triggering a public controversy and negative publicity.

Legal and Copyright Uncertainties

Generative AI automatically collects data from various sources for training, which may be copyrighted or confidential. These risks make companies more cautious when choosing generative AI tools. In addition, the copyright issue of AI-generated content remains unclear, which continues to hinder commercialization.

Example: A technology company showcased a logo developed by AI at a trade show, which led to a lawsuit because the logo contained copyrighted templates. Public pressure forced the company to withdraw the campaign.

Resource and Cost Issues

Training and applying generative AI is highly resource intensive. In particular, small and medium-sized enterprises are faced with limited hardware infrastructure and computing power. In addition, the complex maintenance of the technology increases the demands on technical teams.

Data: According to statistics, pre-training a medium-sized language model can produce more than 300 tons of carbon dioxide emissions, which is equivalent to the total emissions of an intercontinental flight.

Actionable Recommendations to Overcome Barriers and Future Opportunities

Data Management and Algorithm Transparency

Companies should establish more effective data cleaning and pre-processing methods in data collection and use to ensure the legality and diversity of data sources. By adopting advanced transparency technologies such as blockchain or explainable AI algorithms, data quality and credibility can be improved. At the same time, companies should apply industry standards to create more precise data standards for generative AI.

Human-Machine Collaboration as a Control Mechanism

The capabilities of generative AI can be supplemented by hybrid human-machine workflows. Companies should not use AI as a complete substitute for human intervention but establish a collaborative relationship in which human review acts as a control mechanism to ensure that generated content meets cultural and ethical standards. This double safeguard not only reduces risks but also improves the quality of AI-generated results.

Technological Lightweight and Green Optimization

In view of the high cost of resource consumption, companies should focus on developing less costly and lighter generative AI models. Miniaturized edge-computing models and quantized models with shared parameters have already shown potential for reducing resource consumption. At the same time, sustainable energy solutions for training and deployment should be promoted to reduce the carbon footprint.

Proactive Legal Framework

Companies should actively participate in shaping legal and policy frameworks that support the long-term development of the industry, such as introducing profit sharing agreements or marking for AI-generated content. These new guidelines reduce legal risks and create a more innovation-friendly environment for generative AI.

Key to the Future: Balancing Scalability and Responsibility

Generative AI offers exciting future prospects for companies. However, there are still technical challenges and practical limitations that need to be addressed. Companies should not only use this technology to expand their market potential but also take responsibility to promote its transparent and fair development. In the future, generative AI will not only serve as a tool but also act as a core driver of strategic transformation, thereby contributing to the creation of a more intelligent, inclusive, and sustainable global economy.

Chapter 6
Challenges and Limitations Met by Advances and Solutions

The rapid development of artificial intelligence (AI) has brought about profound changes in all areas of human life and business. AI's influence is evident not only in transforming everyday experiences but also in reshaping the operational foundations of organizations across a multitude of sectors.

Revolutionary Value and Existing Limitations

AI applications offer revolutionary added value in many scenarios, enabling new capabilities and efficiencies previously unattainable. However, it is important to recognize that the technology has its boundaries. As AI-driven models become more advanced, new restrictions and barriers are emerging and becoming increasingly visible. These limitations are not confined solely to data and algorithms, but also encompass computational resources, energy consumption, and the time required for processing and implementation.

Visible Barriers and Critical Factors

The growing complexity of AI technologies brings to the forefront several critical challenges. These relate not just to the technical aspects of data handling and algorithm design, but also to the practical realities of resource allocation, including the significant demands on computational power and energy, as well as the time constraints inherent in deploying advanced AI systems.

Sector-Specific Challenges and Opportunities

This chapter discusses application-specific challenges and opportunities presented by AI adoption. The adaptation of AI across various industries demonstrates significant potential for innovation and advancement. By analyzing these sector-specific issues, the discussion aims to highlight both the hurdles and the prospects associated with AI integration.

 | https://doi.org/10.1515/9783112242728-006

Advances, Strategies, and Future Development

Finally, advances in AI, solution strategies, and development paths are presented as ways to harness the potential of addressing critical issues. The focus is on exploring how ongoing progress and targeted approaches can maximize the benefits of AI while managing its inherent limitations.

6.1 Speech Processing and the Interface Revolution

One of the central goals of AI is to make human-machine interaction more natural. Speech processing and natural language processing (NLP) are the key drivers to achieve this goal. These technologies begin with "understanding what is heard" and expand this to "understanding" and "responding."

From Hearing to Understanding: The Next Step of Technology

These technologies change the fundamental ways of executing tasks and redefine the design and use of interfaces. From virtual assistants for everyday household use to complex multi-round dialogue systems, they expand the boundaries of technology and open up new perspectives for developments in professional life, especially in the fields of engineering and management.

In this chapter, the further development of speech processing and NLP technologies is introduced. The central application areas and challenges are analyzed, and ideas for future possibilities are presented.

Development of Speech Recognition: From Keywords to Understanding Contexts

In-depth Technical Analysis and End-to-End Integration in Automatic Speech Recognition

Automatic speech recognition has undergone a shift from modular systems to End-to-End frameworks. Using deep learning models, semantic information is directly extracted from speech signal data. This architecture solves the problem of seamless integration of acoustic models and language models in traditional systems. In particular, the application of Transformer and Conformer models has significantly improved the error resistance of speech recognition to environmental noise and more demanding conversational contexts.

Integration of Semantic Understanding and Language Models

Modern speech recognition systems are no longer limited to stringing words together. By combining with powerful language models (e.g., GPT), they possess dynamic semantic supplementation capabilities. From local language understanding to cloud based collaborations, this semantic sensitivity enables speech technologies to move from "understanding what is heard" to "understanding intentions" and even provide action recommendations.

Applications and Technological Innovations

Revolution in Medical Diagnostic Support

In the medical field, voice-based electronic patient record systems are already widely used, significantly accelerating the documentation processes of doctors. For example, doctors can describe a patient's symptoms by voice while the system searches extensive medical reports and offers solution suggestions.

Dynamic Capture and Analysis of Industrial Data

In industrial manufacturing, speech recognition enables real-time report generation. Technicians can create error reports based on spoken descriptions, and coupled with sensor feedback, the system contributes to error analysis and dynamic production optimization, leading to more efficient processes.

Challenges and Central Points of Tension

Despite technological progress, the following challenges still stand in the way of the comprehensive implementation of speech recognition systems. On the one hand, there is the adaptation to rare languages and accents. The ability of current systems to accurately recognize rare languages and complex accents is still limited. This limitation hampers usage in multicultural contexts and reduces technology accessibility. On the other hand, there are data privacy and technical differences. The sensitive nature of speech data makes data privacy issues particularly critical. It is necessary to design distributed models in edge computing architectures that integrate data processing phases closer to the user side to minimize the risk of data leaks.

Advances in Natural Language Processing: From Dialogues to Contextualization

The development path of the technology goes from the transformation of rule-based to generative models. Traditionally, NLP systems are founded on rule-based approaches, whose effectiveness is still limited when it comes to open and dynamic language needs. Modern generative models (such as GPT or BERT) use extensive amounts of text to develop broad language generalization. In particular, in multi-round dialogues and complex context understanding, these large language models have become indispensable tools in decision making processes.

The processing of language or text alone is increasingly merging with multimodal approaches that also take into account visual or other information. This development offers deeper application possibilities, for example in distance learning or design consulting, and drives the integration of new technologies.

A deeper application possibility lies, for example, in the comprehensive redesign of customer service. NLP improves service by enabling dialogue systems to predict customer needs early. Banking service systems can anticipate further customer questions using predictive language analysis and proactively guide customers to additional service offerings, thereby increasing solution efficiency.

In emergencies, speech and NLP-driven systems can extract immediate information and assist in situation assessment during crises. For example, speech data from passengers in a train accident can directly trigger rescue plans and relay accident information to relevant authorities.

The main technological challenges still lie in uncertainties in dialogue generation. In complex contexts, there is still the risk that NLP models do not accurately interpret the hidden intentions or specific nuances of conversations, especially when it comes to culturally specific matters. The challenge of equality lies in the fact that, due to unequal resource bases, large language models tend to be less effective in supporting languages with low data volumes, which hampers their comprehensive applicability.

Collaboration and Breakthroughs: The Future of Speech Processing

The collaboration between speech recognition and NLP is revolutionizing not only themselves but also opening up new possibilities for engineering and design. The potential applications and opportunities for collaboration seem limitless. Here are some examples:

Smart Vehicles: Combining speech interaction with NLP generation capabilities enables dynamic navigation, integration of traffic resources, and suggestions for drivers, such as avoiding traffic jams.

International Communication: The integration of speech processing and NLP allows for real-time adjustments of translations, which can improve conference interpreting, for example.

Interactive Interfaces: By combining speech, image, and other data sources, more effective design solutions can be created. Users can optimize their interface processes with verbal inputs.

Future innovation opportunities lie in personalized adjustments based on context adaptation. These systems can better follow user behavior and adjust according to previous interactions.

Another innovation is intelligent edge computing. Decentralized analysis and processing processes accelerate real-time application handling speeds and promote data security.

Summary: On the Way to an Unlimited Interaction World

Speech recognition and NLP have already become key technologies for smart interfaces, bringing about groundbreaking changes in engineering, management, and society. Despite challenges such as data privacy and cultural barriers, these technologies are leading the way to a future where human-machine interactions become more intuitive and efficient.

From "tool" to "partnership," speech and NLP technologies are increasingly realizing their potential. With optimizations and further dissemination, we can expect a truly barrier-free world. The understanding between humans and machines is a crucial step toward an intelligent society.

6.2 The Value of AI in Multimodal Interaction Design

Multimodal interaction design plays an indispensable role in innovation management and all AI applications in engineering and management. Its core concept is to integrate visual, tactile, and linguistic input and output forms to enable a more natural and seamless user experience and task processing.

Against the backdrop of the ongoing digitalization of user habits, this interaction mode provides key support for increasing production efficiency and transforming service models across various industries. AI is the key driver in multimodal interaction. With its powerful cognitive abilities and real-time processing performance, devices can autonomously adjust their interaction modes in dynamic and constantly changing environments.

This section explores the value of multimodal interaction design from a technological perspective. By conducting an in-depth analysis of visual, tactile, and linguistic technologies, important application scenarios are highlighted. At the same time, technological pros and cons are presented through real-life examples, and feasible optimization approaches are suggested to provide valuable long-term solutions for technological implementation.

Key Technologies of Multimodal Interaction: Vision, Tactile, and Language

Visual Technology: Promoting Intuitive Data Interaction

The rapid progress in visual recognition technology, supported by deep learning, pattern recognition, and AI algorithms, has fundamentally changed multimodal interaction design. By efficiently capturing and interpreting visual data, industrial devices and smart terminals have gained the ability to understand their surroundings. Examples include:

Identity Verification and Security Measures: Facial recognition for login has become a core application in the field of financial technology. Combined with 3D imaging and dynamic lip motion recognition, it can further minimize the risk of data forgery.

Augmented Reality: In the industrial sector, AR glasses can overlay work instructions and component descriptions in real time onto the actual working environment, reducing human errors and increasing the efficiency of closed loop production.

Personalized Information Offers: Smart cameras analyze user behavior and recommend suitable products, significantly increasing conversion rates in the retail industry.

Visual technologies not only optimize the user experience but also provide valuable data for decision making. However, challenges such as insufficient data privacy and algorithmic biases still exist, especially in facial recognition, which may disadvantage certain user groups. This calls for optimizations at both the technological and policy levels.

Tactile Technology: Enhancing Immersion and Precision

Tactile technologies enable two-way interaction between devices and users through feedback, vibration stimulation, or temperature perception. This tactile technology not only provides a richer interaction experience but is indispensable in scenarios requiring precise movements, such as:

Medical Training Simulations: Tactile simulation systems offer surgeons precise tissue feedback, allowing them to refine their techniques in a virtual environment.

Tactile Smart-Home Experience: Devices with tactile feedback buttons not only enhance user friendliness but also convey information on whether an action has been successfully executed through differentiated force feedback.

Industrial Robots with Tactile Sensors: Robots can identify material properties using tactile sensors and perform appropriate work processes based on this, such as safely handling sensitive objects in complex environments.

Challenges in the field of tactile interaction technology mainly involve high hardware costs and limited sensor precision. This demands technological innovation and the development of sustainable business models to improve the cost benefit ratio.

Language Technology: Driving Natural Communication

NLP and speech recognition are essential components of multimodal interaction. They enable devices to understand human language at various levels, from executing simple instructions to managing complex interactions. Examples include:

- Expansion of Voice Assistant Functions: Smart voice assistants are no longer limited to functions such as music playback or weather forecasting but also support a wider range of tasks such as travel planning or household budget management, saving users' time.
- Real-Time Speech Recording and Analysis: In healthcare, doctors' speech recordings can be directly converted into electronic medical records, increasing data management efficiency.
- Interactive Speech Translation: Speech translation systems can enable real-time multilingual communication in international business situations, easily overcoming language barriers.

The complexity of language-based interaction design lies in the ability to accurately interpret dynamic contexts and linguistic differences. To achieve broader and more equitable coverage, AI development needs to focus on reducing models that contain cultural or linguistic biases.

Collaboration of Key Technologies: Synergistic Innovation in Multimodal Interaction

The special value of multimodal interaction design lies in the integration of AI technologies to create a unified experience. This value is particularly evident in complex scenarios, such as:

- Inclusive Design for Assistive Applications: Devices combine verbal descriptions with visual analysis to provide real-time information about the environment to visually impaired individuals. Tactile feedback further assists in locating objects or confirming their distance.
- Dynamic Work Processes: In the smart home, the central control system monitors environmental influences using visual technologies, communicates with users through speech, and provides haptic feedback via control panels to precisely support decision making.
- Collaborative Industry 4.0 Applications: Intelligent robots combine visual recognition, tactile sensors, and verbal instructions into a coherent interaction system that efficiently performs complex tasks such as precision work in high temperature environments.

The added value of these collaborative technologies lies not only in the mutual complementarity of capabilities but also in the overarching optimization of work processes and user experiences. In this way, AI becomes a central driver of multimodal interaction design.

Exemplified Analyses

Example 1: Assistive Remote Diagnosis Systems in Autonomous Driving

In the field of intelligent mobility, multimodal interaction design has fundamentally changed the safety and control mechanisms in vehicles:

Visual Technology: Cameras analyze road conditions in real time, detect pedestrians or obstacles, and provide precise route recommendations for autonomous driving.

Tactile Technology: The system uses vibrations in the steering wheel to warn of lane departures or potential collisions, alerting the driver to potential dangers and reducing reaction time.

Verbal Technology: The system not only processes the driver's voice commands but also provides feedback in a dynamic environment, such as verbal tips on driving conditions in snow and rain.

This example shows how technological synergies in complex scenarios not only increase safety but also create more personalized and comfortable user experiences.

Example 2: Intelligent Learning Aids Through Multimodal Interaction

In the field of education, multimodal interaction design expands the possibilities of traditional learning approaches through the integration of AI technologies:

Visual Technology: Learning platforms analyze students' facial expressions and body posture to assess their attention levels and dynamically adjust learning methods.

Tactile Technology: Visually impaired students use tactile feedback devices to learn Braille, increasing learning efficiency. Vibrational feedback on learning platforms helps children improve their reading concentration.

Verbal Technology: Voice assistants act as virtual tutors, guiding students through the learning process with interactive dialogues. Voice translation tools also facilitate the learning of new foreign languages.

The use of multimodal technologies makes learning more personalized and broadens educational opportunities, driving the democratization of technology in the education sector.

Technological Development Bottlenecks and Implementation Strategies

Despite the obvious advantages of multimodal interaction technologies, there are central challenges in widespread application:

Interoperability: The integration of different technologies requires standardized industry solutions to reduce development costs and improve system compatibility.

Data Privacy and Ethics: Multimodal interactions require the processing of large amounts of data. It is essential to ensure both data integrity and privacy protection.

Hardware Costs and Accessibility: High-precision visual and tactile hardware is currently very expensive. To expand access, cost-effective manufacturing processes and targeted innovation approaches are needed.

Future breakthroughs will depend on comprehensive cross-industry collaboration and in-depth ethical reflection. Additionally, the introduction of edge computing and the development of lightweight AI algorithms could help reduce application barriers and promote the marketability of these technologies.

Conclusion: Shaping a Digital Ecosystem for Interaction

AI-supported multimodal interaction design redefines the boundaries of human-machine communication. By integrating visual, tactile, and verbal technologies, not only are more natural interaction environments created, but new impetus is also given in areas such as business, education, and healthcare.

In the future, efficient and coordinated multimodal interaction will not only be a tool for technological innovation but also a key driver for social inclusion and justice. The rational confrontation with implementation challenges and a holistic understanding of user requirements will ultimately determine whether this technology can pave the way for society into a smarter and more equitable digital future.

6.3 User Data Protection and Interactive Security

With the continuous optimization of intelligent interactions, we are enjoying increasingly convenient and efficient digital experiences. However, we stand at a crossroads between the protection of privacy and data security. AI relies on the collection and processing of vast amounts of information, such as user behavior, voice commands, or emotional data, which serve as the foundation for designing and optimizing interactive interfaces. But like a double-edged sword, the massive flow of data contributes to technological development on one hand, while posing significant risks to privacy and security on the other.

The Value of Data and the Dilemma of Security

Balancing user privacy and technological expansion in interaction design has become an essential challenge of our time. Protecting privacy in intelligent interfaces not only requires higher technical standards but also poses a serious test for ethical responsibility and political frameworks.

In the following, we systematically analyze this issue from three perspectives: data-technical strategies, legal support, and ecological and ethical innovations. In addition, suggestions are made for future oriented, privacy friendly interaction designs to create a safer and more sustainable environment for intelligent interactions.

Data-Technical Challenges in Intelligent Interactions

Intelligent interaction interfaces serve as a dialogue platform between users and devices, focusing on analyzing user needs and delivering precise feedback. However, behind this close relationship lie numerous data protection and security issues that urgently need to be resolved.

Abuse and Lack of Transparency in Data Collection

Designing intelligent interactions requires extensive user data, including behavior patterns, location data, conversation content, and even emotional reactions. This data-driven approach allows for almost complete insights into users' lives. However, the following problems arise:

Lack of Transparency: Users often cannot understand which data is collected, for what purpose, and whether it might be shared or sold. Many terms of use are hard to understand, further exacerbating information asymmetry.

Standardized Data Sharing: Some interfaces allow data access by default and treat users as potential data providers without sufficiently communicating their explicit consent or options. This "technological dictatorship" is increasingly undermining user trust.

Potential Risks of Data Leaks

User data is stored on local servers or in the cloud, and its quantity and value make it a preferred target for cyberattacks. Several data breaches worldwide have already raised serious security concerns. Key issues here are:

Vulnerabilities During Transmission: Data transmission between devices relies on the reliability of encryption protocols, which provides a potential attack surface for manipulations.

Centralized Risks in Cloud Storage: Although cloud storage solutions facilitate synchronization, their centralized structure often attracts more attacks.

Algorithmic Biases and Unequal Data Processing

AI is highly dependent on the quality of data on which its algorithms are trained. Algorithmic biases can not only affect the usability of interfaces but also raise ethical and legal concerns:

Biased Data Transfer: Gender-specific, ethnic, or cultural biases can be favored in the design process of intelligent systems due to the existing input data.

Misinterpretations of Behavior: For example, emotional AI systems might mistakenly interpret anger and raise concerns about controlling technology through inappropriate feedback.

Breakthrough in Privacy-Oriented Design

Modern interaction design must resolve the conflict between functionality and data protection. While user data should be handled safely and transparently, control capabilities and user experience must not be neglected. Here are some essential approaches:

Principle of Data Minimization: Slim Design, Targeted Permissions

The core idea of slim design is to limit data collection to essential functions without gathering unnecessary information. On-demand retrievals and time-limited data usage could transform data records into a transparent service.

Example: Technologies such as "end-to-end encryption" with locally stored analysis data are already in use. This is best demonstrated in health apps that adopt strict user authorization mechanisms.

Local Computing and Encrypted Transmission

Optimization can be achieved through edge computing. Speech recognition or facial analysis data processing takes place on local devices, reducing dependence on cloud services. This minimizes transmission risks and security concerns of centralized storage.

Example: In the context of the GDPR, many companies have adapted their AI models to perform calculations on end devices.

Encrypted transmissions ensure data security through end-to-end encryption, and the use of blockchain technology is employed for verification. This guarantees that only authorized recipients can decrypt the data.

User Friendliness and Control Options

Transparency in interactions is also important. Users should be able to clearly understand how data is processed through the interface and what feedback is generated by AI. Interactive interfaces should also serve to help users understand the value of data protection. Through dynamic design, symbols can be displayed to show the data flow and permission status in real time. With built-in user control, one should be able to edit, delete, or withdraw their data at any time, instead of passively letting technology manage it.

Legal Support Through Framework Conditions

Technology-based data protection requires strict legal oversight. Some important measures and proposals are international standards. These range from the General Data Protection Regulation (GDPR) to the California Consumer Privacy Act (CCPA) and set standards in terms of data transparency:

- Data usage in the GDPR context: Intelligent interfaces must explicitly seek user feedback on data usage and also offer dynamic decision making options.
- Complaint mechanism of the CCPA: Tracking systems for data processing allow users to check traceability and feedback options.

Showcase Model of Federated Learning

Limiting data exchange does not automatically mean stopping it completely. Decentralized approaches like federated learning enable cooperation without full data sharing. The basic principle here consists of decentralized machine learning units, where data remains local while model parameters are updated.

The Path to Higher Security and Intelligent Technologies

Data protection is not a brake on development. On the contrary, it is more about technology security combined with visible methods.

In the practical application of AI, technology has made significant progress but still faces multidimensional limitations. The four central challenges include data quality, computational power requirements, ethical controversies, and sectoral isolation. These issues hinder the broad implementation and value of the technology. In the area of data quality, the development of AI is highly dependent on high-quality training data, a dependency that is restricted by data protection laws, data silos, and the lack of cross-industry standards. A case in point is the medical sector, where AI systems cannot achieve true generalization ability due to the absence of mechanisms for data exchange between institutions. To address this challenge, current research focuses on promoting standardized data protocols and data protection technologies (such as federated learning) to balance the tension between data protection and data availability.

Computational Power and Ecological Innovation

Another important factor that limits the continuous expansion of AI is the consumption of resources and computational power. Today's complex models (especially generative AI) require immense computational resources, which not only drive up development costs but also raise concerns about the sustainability of energy consumption. This issue calls for research approaches that not only include algorithmic optimization and model compression but also target hardware infrastructures that focus on sustainable computing. More efficient chip technologies and decentralized computer architectures could mitigate the challenges in resource management.

Ethical Innovations

When it comes to ethics and social responsibility, the lack of transparency in decision making and the trustworthiness of results are paramount. The "black box" phenomenon of AI makes the results difficult to explain, and the use of biased data can further exacerbate social inequalities. Particularly in critical areas such as health and justice, these issues cannot be ignored. Future solutions require the development of transparent and explainable algorithms that embed ethical considerations into the model development process. Complemented by standardized evaluation mechanisms, this can strengthen societal trust.

Sectoral Isolation

Sectoral fragmentation and the phenomenon of technology silos hinder the comprehensive utilization of AI's potential across various fields. Many cutting-edge technologies remain confined to specific sectors due to the lack of systemic support for cross-industry collaboration. For example, the expansion of medical imaging technologies to industrial inspection processes through open ecosystems and technology exchange platforms could unleash higher innovation power. Despite current challenges, AI shows tremendous development potential. From fundamental theory to innovative technologies at the research frontier (such as the intersection of quantum computing and neuroscience), groundbreaking breakthroughs could be achieved in the future.

Moreover, promoting global collaboration in developing a technology-steering governance framework in the political and ethical domain will create a safer and more resilient environment for AI development. These multifaceted efforts will not only overcome current obstacles in technology application but also promote social value creation through AI. Ultimately, AI, as an integrating element of technology, management, and social mechanisms, will enable a fairer and more sustainable social transformation.

6.4 Technological Progress and Limits: The Unreachable Areas of AI

As AI-driven models deepen, these limits become increasingly clear. From computational requirements to data issues, from algorithm development to ethical challenges, each stage poses insurmountable resistances and hurdles.

In this section, we will address the core problems of these technological expansions and discuss how technological and societal harmony can be achieved despite existing limitations.

Computational Power and Algorithm Optimization: A Tense Balancing Act Against Efficiency Bottlenecks

Today's deep learning and generative AI models require unprecedented computational power, which has also rapidly driven and will continue to drive the development of hardware technologies. However, this dependence on high computational power creates a series of technological and resource-related imbalances. The discrepancy between increasing computational power and optimized algorithms is one of the central obstacles preventing AI from overcoming existing performance limits.

Hardware Limitations: The Pressure of High-Performance Computing Requirements

The computational demand of deep learning shows exponential growth. For example, deeply nested convolutional neural networks in image generation models require tens of thousands of iterations, for which enormous computational resources from GPUs (graphics processing units) are needed. With the further growth of model sizes, the improvement rates of GPUs and TPUs (tensor processing units) will hardly keep up with the exponential increase in computational requirements.

The Pressure for "Green" Computing Methods: The High Energy Consumption in Training Large AI Models

The high energy consumption in training large AI models has brought sustainability issues into focus. For instance, the power consumption of training a large language model is equivalent to the weekly energy consumption of a small city. This calls for breakthroughs in hardware energy efficiency or suitable alternative technologies.

Quantum Computing: The Stealthy Aspirant of the Future

Theoretically, quantum computing can significantly increase efficiency. However, it remains a future vision until its commercialization and widespread use, and thus has no direct impact on AI performance limits.

New Paths for Algorithm Optimization: Integration of Lightweight and Efficiency

Current algorithm optimization mainly focuses on increasing model size (e.g., number of parameters) to improve result performance. However, this approach leads to a significant increase in both computational costs and complexity, creating a "resource dilemma." Further progress in efficiency optimization may require groundbreaking innovations at the kernel level, the core of the operating system.

Opportunities for Parameter Compression

Future approaches should focus more on reducing redundant model parameters and thus lowering resource consumption. For example, pruning in the context of explainable AI can help reduce model size while ensuring stable performance. Pruning in machine learning refers to the simplification, shortening, and optimization of decision trees.

Design of Lightweight Models

Recent developments, such as Meta's lightweight language models like LLaMA (Large Language Model Meta AI), demonstrate the potential to achieve high performance with less data and limited computational resources. Such methods pave the way for AI applications in environments with low computational capacity.

Data Bottlenecks: Rigid Supply Systems and Possible Breakthroughs

Data-drivenness is the core of AI, but the data supply chain is complicated and full of challenges in several phases. Both the quality and acquisition of data and the fragmentation of the data industry pose significant barriers to technological progress through data availability.

The Problem of Adequate Utilization of Data Resources

The development of AI is highly dependent on high-quality data, but this dependency faces numerous limits in practice. The fragmentation and limited shareability of data create particular hurdles.

Data Protection and Regulation

For example, medical data in many countries is subject to strict data protection laws, which significantly restrict cross-regional collaboration and the training of models for intelligent diagnostics.

Challenge of Data Bias

Data bias remains a significant challenge globally. Many generative AI models rely heavily on Western text corpora, making them less effective in other linguistic or cultural contexts.

Data Quality: From Quantity to Accuracy

Although the global amount of data is growing exponentially, a large proportion of this data is of low quality or in unstructured form. This further increases the costs and difficulties in AI development.

Bottlenecks in Automated Data Annotation

Although tools for data cleaning and annotation are becoming more sophisticated, the costs and complexities remain a significant challenge in some dynamic data scenarios (e.g., autonomous driving).

Management of Dynamic Data

Delays and quality degradation in real time data capture affect the acceptance of AI in some sensitive scenarios (e.g., financial transactions). A significant improvement in dynamic data management is urgently needed.

Possible Solutions

Artificially Generated Data (Synthetic Data)

AI could create high-quality simulated data using generative adversarial networks and other artificial methods to compensate for data shortages.

Federated Learning: A Breakthrough for Cross-Industry Collaboration

Federated learning finds a balance between data protection and data distribution, contributing to increased data utilization efficiency by overcoming sectoral standardization barriers.

Technological Ethics and Cultural Limits: The Untouchable Areas

Technological development is not only characterized by hard limits but also deeply intertwined with ethical and sociocultural aspects. Such soft restrictions can become insurmountable barriers for technological expansion.

Transparency of Decisions and Accountability

Many AI applications face the problem of the "black box": The decision making logic remains hidden in the algorithm, causing users to lose trust in the results.

Transparency Needs in Key Areas

Particularly in the financial and health sectors, algorithm transparency and explainability are crucial for integrating AI into the legal and moral frameworks of these industries.

Societal Fairness and Accountability Dilemmas

When data bias leads to discriminatory or differentiated results, accountability often becomes the subject of societal debates.

Irreplaceable Human Domains

Although AI excels in areas such as language processing and pattern recognition, it cannot replace human creativity, ethical judgment, and complex collaboration. Main issues are:

Uniqueness of Creativity and Innovation: Human artistic inspiration and philosophical contemplation cannot be encoded for the time being and remain key areas that AI cannot penetrate.

Cultural and Emotional Dimensions: Emotional AI still struggles to comprehensively understand the complexity of cultures and human psychology. Further progress in these areas is necessary and feasible.

Future Oriented Paths to Overcoming Limits

Collaboration of all stakeholders, social responsibility, and careful data handling are inevitable to find ways to overcome limits:

Interdisciplinary Collaboration: Integrating research from engineering, social sciences, psychology, and other fields promotes the multidimensional expansion of technology.

Ethics and Responsibility in the Design Phase: Ethical considerations and humanistic approaches should be included during development to give AI development deeper social significance.

International Data Usage Rules: It is essential to create global data cooperation standards based on standardization and promote sustainable open data platforms.

Conclusion: Managing Technical Boundaries in Expansion

The tensions between technical expansion and its boundaries are not simple opposites but a dynamic balance and coexistence. These challenges shape not only the pace of technological development but also foster closer collaboration between industries, society, and disciplines. From innovation to ethics, from computational power to data, AI will continue to experiment at these boundaries and redefine its developmental paths to enable a harmonious coexistence of technology and human society.

6.5 Challenges and Opportunities in the Use of AI Across Industries

When AI is applied to specific industries, its potential impact is often intertwined with the complexity of practical implementation. From a cross-industry perspective, it is clear that while the general technical capabilities of AI are steadily increasing, adapting these capabilities to specific industry scenarios is fraught with significant challenges.

Risks and Conflicts in Technical Expansion

This section examines the issues of industry adaptation of AI, including limited data resources, insufficient algorithm specificity, and conflicts of interest among various parties. From case studies to practical approaches, solutions are explored, and new possibilities for overcoming adaptation bottlenecks are considered through a look at trends.

Core Barriers in Industry Application

Data Resource Issues: The development and application of AI are unimaginable without a solid data foundation. However, in industry scenarios, accessing data, processing it, and exchanging it is a formidable obstacle. The uneven distribution of structured and unstructured data within an industry sector, coupled with restrictions from data protection laws, makes obtaining high-quality data a central challenge that hinders the expansion of AI applications.

Data Protection Barriers in Healthcare: For instance, in the healthcare industry, AI-assisted image analysis requires models that can accurately identify patient anomalies. This necessitates extensive, cross-institutional image datasets. However, data protection regulations such as the GDPR (General Data Protection Regulation) (EU) or HIPAA (Health Insurance Portability and Accountability Act) (USA) even block data integration between hospitals. AI projects in healthcare often encounter diagnostic biases, for example, due to the lack of data from Asian patients in certain training datasets, which significantly affects global application accuracy.

Challenges in Algorithm Transfer: AI algorithms often rely on universal technological concepts, while specific industry applications require specialized knowledge. Seamlessly transferring standard algorithms to vertical industry scenarios is difficult because adapting to industry-specific characteristics requires substantial financial and time investments, complicating rapid amortization.

Industrial Applications and Sectoral Transferability Issues: For example, industrial automation is increasingly adopting intelligent visual technologies. However, AI-based visual inspections face difficulties due to different data requirements and problem characteristics. An AI defect detection model for automotive production lines cannot be easily applied to bottling lines in beverage production. The process of understanding industry-specific characteristics not only extends implementation time but also leads to significantly higher costs, creating a gap between actual benefits and costs.

Skill Shortages and Technological Barriers: The successful integration of AI into industry applications requires interdisciplinary talents who are proficient in both AI technology and industry-specific knowledge. However, there is a severe global shortage of highly qualified professionals with this dual expertise. Moreover, collaboration between industry specialists and AI experts is often hindered by communication problems and competency gaps.

Challenges in the Education Sector: Compared to sectors such as healthcare or manufacturing, the application of AI in education is still in an experimental phase. Despite the promising potential of personalized learning recommendations and predictive analytics, progress is hampered by the lack of professionals who can effectively translate the specific advantages of AI into practice. As a result, many projects remain limited to pilot studies. At the same time, cost pressures and the absence of funding models act as additional brakes on the establishment of large-scale AI solutions.

Legal Restrictions and Lack of Transparency: The characteristics of AI are increasingly in tension with legal and ethical boundaries. In data-intensive industries such as finance and healthcare, legal requirements complicate the introduction of AI, because transparency and reliability become central challenges for the technology. For example, algorithms used for risk assessment face regulatory scrutiny due to their lack of explainability.

Transparency Issues in the Financial Sector: The financial industry sees AI as a tool for simplifying credit risk assessments and fraud detection. However, opaque "black box" models hinder the adoption of the technology because regulatory authorities fear a loss of control due to unexplainable processes. For instance, an AI system used by an international bank to evaluate complex financial instruments was ultimately rejected by regulators because the information risks were deemed unacceptable.

Solution Strategies and Development Opportunities

Combining Data Protection and Data Sharing: A key to overcoming data-sharing barriers lies in maximizing the value of data within a legally permissible framework while protecting privacy. Technologies like federated learning enable different actors to jointly train models without revealing the original data.

New Approaches for Intersectoral Collaboration in Healthcare: A technology company collaborating with a US hospital network provided a federated learning solution that consolidated data from various sites to create a diagnostic model covering the entire patient population. As a result, the model's accuracy was significantly improved without violating regulations. This example highlights the potential of privacy-preserving computations, thereby enhancing both the general acceptance and efficiency of AI models.

Industry Knowledge as a Driver of AI Transformation

The integration of AI capabilities with deep industry knowledge can significantly enhance the sectoral adaptability of AI. One approach is to incorporate technical, medical, personal, physical, or industry-specific insights into the training logic of AI, also known as knowledge-guided machine learning. This reduces the dependence on extensive experimental datasets.

Examples of this can be seen in the energy sector. To predict complex power grid loads, a research team developed an AI model that directly embeds physical insights into the algorithm logic. This enabled the creation of a reliable model with minimal data requirements. This method offers a pioneering solution for all resource-poor industries.

Promoting a Collaborative Data Ecosystem

A key way to overcome data isolation within AI applications is to create collaborative and cross-industry data and technology platforms. Standardizing interfaces and open data standards can significantly contribute to making industry-specific AI solutions interoperable and more efficiently usable.

Success with Open Data in Agriculture: In the field of precision farming, US and European agricultural machinery manufacturers signed a cooperation agreement to create common interface standards for AI applications. This unification enabled seamless integration of monitoring systems for plant irrigation and weather forecasting, significantly increasing the innovation speed and market penetration in agriculture.

Future Trends and Potentials for New Adaptation Forms

With the ongoing development of technologies and political frameworks, the adaptation of AI to industry requirements will be facilitated by the following trends:

Real-Time Learning with Small Datasets: Advances in few-shot learning and transfer learning will enable broader industry adaptation with minimal data effort and lower costs.

Cooperative Regulation: AI-supported systems could actively participate in the development of intelligent regulation, bringing more flexibility and dynamics into the legal framework through algorithmic evaluation models.

Open-Source Ecosystems: Every opening of AI algorithms in open-source format will significantly lower entry barriers for small and medium-sized enterprises and promote diversity in the use of AI technologies.

Conclusion

The adaptation of AI to specific industries is not an insurmountable hurdle but a continuous effort to create a new balance between expertise and technology. With approaches such as federated learning, knowledge-guided algorithms, and collaborative platform architectures, AI has already demonstrated its capability to transform traditional industries. As legal and technological frameworks continue to evolve, more and more industries will have the opportunity to benefit from AI, explore entirely new fields of innovation, and shape a truly intelligent future.

6.6 Unlocking Global Potential of Cross-Industry Collaboration

AI technologies are revolutionizing global industry, business, and societal structures at an unprecedented speed. Faced with increasingly complex global markets and technological ecosystems, cross-industry collaboration has become a strategic necessity to overcome niche existence and individual industry barriers and to accelerate innovation.

The Value of Cross-Industry Cooperation in Our Time

By using AI for new communication pathways, not only is the efficiency, scaling, and cost degradation in industry increased, but also the sustainable development of society is supported.

This section examines from a global perspective the mechanisms of cross-industry cooperation potential and analyzes successful approaches as well as challenges. It shows how AI can be the driving force behind cooperative innovation.

Mechanisms and Drivers of Cross-Industry Collaboration with AI

The emergence of cross-industry cooperation is no accident but is based on several important mechanisms and drivers:

Shared Data Competence: AI is based on data, and data from different industries often complement each other excellently. For example, granular consumer data from retail can optimize the models of credit assessment in the financial sector, while risk data from the financial sector, in turn, improves forecasts in retail.

Technological Penetration and Efficiency Improvement: By complementarily using AI technologies, industries can quickly increase their efficiency. For example, AI-supported automation from the manufacturing industry is used in the medical field to promote the development of high-precision devices and the standardization of medical procedures.

Demand-Oriented Cooperative Relationships: With the increasing dependence of industries on intelligent systems, traditional individual solutions can no longer meet the complex requirements. Cross-industry cooperation leads to integrated approaches that solve numerous problems simultaneously and bring decisive advantages in global competition.

These cooperation mechanisms not only promote technological innovation but also open up a variety of application possibilities for AI, making the boundaries between different industries increasingly permeable and flexible.

Practical Examples and Insights of Cross-Industry Collaboration

Precision Medicine and Intelligent Manufacturing

The collaboration between the medical industry and the manufacturing sector has led to groundbreaking advancements in precision medicine. The combination of AI and 3D printing technology from manufacturing enables the personalized design of medical devices such as orthopedic implants, tailored specifically to the needs of patients. Moreover, advanced quality control from the manufacturing industry enhances the reliability of medical devices. A leading international medical robotics company benefits from such collaboration, allowing microsurgical instruments to be marketed more quickly and simultaneously establishing standards in the medical field.

Agriculture and Environmental Sciences: Integration of Resources

The technical integration between agriculture and environmental sciences creates a new ecological network. AI-supported environmental sensors and satellite imagery help farmers monitor soil fertility and climate changes in real time and optimize their planting methods as well as the use of fertilizers. This not only increases agricultural efficiency but also reduces environmental pollution from chemical fertilizers. A demonstration project shows that AI-assisted soil data analysis increased agricultural yields by 15% while significantly reducing water consumption.

Technological Integration of Retail and Financial Services

The cooperation between the retail and financial sectors is a classic example of cross-industry collaboration. The financial sector optimized payment security for retail platforms using AI-based risk management methods, while the retail sector developed better credit assessment models using consumer behavior data. These data-driven technological integrations significantly enhanced user experience. For example, a retail digital payment network with an integrated bank rewards model allows customers to execute various payment methods through a single interface and simultaneously receive personalized service recommendations.

Technological Bottlenecks and Solutions in Cross-Industry Collaboration

Secure Management of High-Dimensional Data

Data sharing is the foundation of cross-industry collaboration, but the secure handling of high-dimensional data remains a significant challenge. Particularly in highly data-sensitive areas such as medicine and finance, any security breach can have serious consequences. Possible solutions include:

Application of Differential Privacy and Federated Learning: Using differential privacy technologies to secure user information so that even if model interfaces are opened, the raw data cannot be directly restored. Federated learning allows AI models to utilize distributed data without data exchange.

Integration of Blockchain Technology: Building a cross-industry network using blockchain where all data accesses are transparently and immutably recorded in the distributed ledger.

Technological Adaptation Between Industries

Different technological requirements make cross-industry integration difficult. For example, the manufacturing industry relies on hardware technologies, while the retail industry increasingly implements software solutions. Solutions include:

Modular Technology Development: AI technologies should be designed in a modular way to be flexibly adapted to the infrastructure of different industries. For example, AI-supported image processing systems can be used for quality control in manufacturing as well as for consumer behavior analysis in retail.

Optimization of Open-Source Platforms: Promoting the development of open-source AI algorithms for cross-industry adaptation so that users can quickly customize AI solutions without incurring high costs or time losses.

Challenges Posed by Business Models and Cultural Differences

Global cross-industry collaborations are often limited by different business models and cultures. For example, developed countries often prefer subscription services, while developing countries tend to choose one-time purchase options. Recommended solutions include:

Data-Driven Global Business Decisions: Using AI to analyze the behavior of customers from different cultural backgrounds and develop optimized business models based on this.

International Multi-party Agreements: Creating a cross-industry collaboration alliance that serves as an independent platform to coordinate global cooperation and establish unified rules for cross-border collaboration.

Strategic Positioning: Building a Global Technology Ecosystem

Establishing Cross-Industry Open-Source Labs and Research Institutes

Global AI research labs should bring together experts from industries such as medicine, agriculture, and manufacturing to create experimental platforms for cross-industry technologies. For example, Microsoft's "AI for Earth" project successfully promotes cooperation between different industries and provides technological support for sustainable development. This model not only accelerates the innovation process but also balances regional resource differences.

Developing AI-Based Industry Ecosystems

The ultimate goal of cross-industry collaboration is not only technology transfer but also the formation of intelligent industry ecosystems. A successful ecosystem includes networked solutions, key links in the supply chain, and shared technological resources. For example, an AI-supported ecosystem involving agriculture, the financial sector, and the consumer goods industry could provide integrated support, from agricultural technology to financial assistance to marketing.

Ethics and Social Responsibility in Collaboration

Ethical issues cannot be ignored in global collaborations. The establishment of a cross-industry and politically independent ethics oversight institute, as well as the development of internationally applicable AI standards, can minimize risks and make collaboration accessible to all. For example, the International AI Ethics Committee is currently exploring the concept of a fair technology use agreement, which ensures that cross-industry AI cooperation does not further marginalize disadvantaged groups.

Conclusion: From Collaboration to Global Innovation

Cross-industry collaboration is the key to unlocking the potential of AI. By cooperating in the areas of data, technology, and business strategy, not only are barriers between industries overcome, but new global innovation models are also created.

The future focus lies in promoting a secure, open, and sustainable cooperation ecosystem as the central mission of AI. This enables various sectors to effectively tackle complex challenges. With the increasing steps of globalization, the potential of cross-industry AI cooperation will not only support technological progress but also contribute to comprehensive economic and social improvements. The expansion of global ecosystems aims to create a connected, intelligent world with AI as the cornerstone.

6.7 Latest Achievements and Future Potential

The continuous progress of AI is driving profound changes in all areas of everyday and professional life in society. Its applications have gone far beyond the original research projects and are now a key driver for industry and the economy.

A Multidimensional Future Through Artificial Intelligence

From optimizing resources to promoting business model innovation, AI has given unprecedented impetus to social, organizational, and individual processes. However, the rapid development of this technology also brings new challenges, including ethical controversies, unequal resource allocation, and the issue of technological regionalization.

This section provides a review of the current achievements of AI applications in various scenarios, analyzes central conflicts, and examines the potential and direction of further AI development through globalization and cross-industry intersections.

Review: Current Results of AI Practice

Health and Medicine: From Diagnoses to Intelligent Treatment

The introduction of AI is revolutionizing traditional medical procedures. From the early days of supporting diagnoses to personalized treatments, AI has become a key driver of precision medicine. For example, deep learning medical imaging platforms have significantly improved the accuracy and efficiency of early disease detection, such as cancer and retinal diseases. In addition, AI algorithms enable personalized treatment plans based on the analysis of genomic data and electronic patient records.

However, a central challenge remains: the so-called "data silo effect" in healthcare, as sensitive patient data restricts the cross-sector and cross-border use of models. Moreover, the use of AI in medically underserved areas is still limited, which requires broader technical inclusion.

Intelligent Industry: Flexible Manufacturing and Dynamic Supply Chains

The industry is experiencing an AI-driven revolution. Intelligent production lines have significantly increased production efficiency and quality control. By combining the Industrial Internet of Things (IIoT) with AI-controlled systems, companies can now respond flexibly to demand fluctuations and interruptions in logistics. AI-supported predictive models also optimize inventory and shipping, allowing companies to save significantly on operating costs.

However, small and medium-sized enterprises (SMEs) often face resource and competence issues. The more effective integration of value chains and the establishment of systematic industry standards are long-term challenges.

Generative AI: Comprehensive Solutions from Creativity to Application

The explosive development of generative AI technology is fundamentally changing the creative economy. Text and image generation models are already widely used in advertising, game development, and film production. Their individuality and efficiency greatly enrich the creative industry. At the same time, generative AI improves business processes through applications such as report generation and documentation automation.

However, these technologies also pose risks. The spread of false information and copyright issues are potential challenges. Therefore, it is essential to create guidelines for ethics and management in connection with generative AI and increase the transparency of processes.

Intelligent Service Ecosystem: From Individual Technologies to Multimodal Integration

AI is transforming the entire service industry based on NLP, emotional computing, and user behavior analysis. In areas such as education and finance, companies are increasingly using intelligent assistants and emotional recognition technologies to optimize human-machine interfaces. This not only improves the user experience but also completely restructures entire service processes.

However, technological limitations continue to pose a barrier to widespread use. Language processing errors in multicultural contexts and inaccuracies in emotion recognition can lead to misinterpretations. Data protection requirements also make the broader introduction of such technologies more difficult.

Core Conflicts in the Implementation of Artificial Intelligence

Data Silos and Limited Cross-Sector Data Exchange

Despite the enormous potential of AI, data barriers between industries, institutions, and states hinder the synergistic use of these technologies. Particularly in data-intensive sectors such as healthcare and finance, large-scale data exchanges are limited by legal and security issues. Promoting technologies such as federated learning and privacy computing is a crucial step in tackling the problem of data silos.

Algorithmic Biases and the Fairness Dilemma

AI models are often influenced by algorithmic biases in the underlying data, leading to unjustified prejudices that can exacerbate existing social inequalities in society. Particularly in sensitive areas such as hiring processes and credit assessments, this can lead to the disadvantage of certain groups. Solving this problem requires both improved data preparation and model optimization, and should be supported by policy measures.

Adaptation Problems in Human-Machine Collaboration

The integration of AI not only changes traditional workflows but also encounters resistance in employee acceptance. Moreover, complex adaptation processes extend the time span in which measurable business gains can be realized. Tailored training and technology concepts that meet the needs of different hierarchical levels are central points here.

Technological Potential and Strategic Perspectives

Cross-Industry Cooperation: Promoting Multimodal Application Scenarios

The future development of AI will increasingly overcome the boundaries of traditional industries by relying on technology recycling and resource synergies. For example, AI and renewable energy in the logistics sector can not only optimize transportation routes but also reduce energy costs. In the education sector, intelligent learning programs can be combined with precise medical management systems to address mental health issues. The breakthrough of such interdisciplinary approaches will shape the next development cycle of AI.

Technological Openness: Building an Open-Source Ecosystem

The further spread of AI will strongly depend on technological openness and standardization. Open models and transparent technological documentation could help SMEs reduce learning and application barriers. At the same time, the combination of encryption and distributed computing technologies can protect sensitive data and promote cross-border innovations.

Public Governance: Strengthening Ethics and International Governance

As AI proliferates, questions of ethics and governance become increasingly pressing. Nations should advance global initiatives to regulate data privacy, algorithmic transparency, and fairness in technology application. Institutions like the United Nations or international technology alliances could promote the establishment of global AI ethics committees. In the long term, such governance structures will lay the foundation for global technological justice and cooperation.

Social Responsibility: Promoting Social Sustainability with AI

AI has the potential to maximize social responsibility in areas such as agriculture, education, and climate protection. AI platforms for agricultural optimization can boost food production and minimize resource waste through dynamic monitoring. Meanwhile, educational models developed for regions with limited technological access can provide high-quality learning resources and close knowledge gaps. These technologies not only drive social progress but also foster a harmonious future for society in line with ecological goals.

Conclusion: Shaping the Future of AI

The development of AI is both a result of technological breakthroughs and a consequence of conscious social shaping. It has become a core driving force for the future of industries, economic structures, and social development. Its evolutionary direction is closely linked to the balance between technological innovation and ethical responsibility.

Looking ahead to the coming years, AI will increasingly be integrated into our daily lives, economy, and social structures. Based on openness, cooperation, and a sense of responsibility, we can work toward a smarter and more equitable world.

Chapter 7
Conclusion and Outlook

In personal life, artificial intelligence (AI) has already permeated every corner of our existence, from smart home automation systems to health and fitness monitoring devices, and on to personalized recommendations and emotional companion functions. These technologies offer unparalleled convenience and efficiency. Compatibility problems between intelligent devices can also affect the user experience, while the danger of data leaks can endanger user privacy and security. As we enjoy the benefits of these technologies, we must also analyze their potential risks from a systemic perspective and seek scientific and inclusive technological governance.

In the professional realm, AI has become deeply embedded and a driving force for cross-industry transformation. It not only accelerates the replacement of mechanized tasks but also introduces new demands for professional skills and competencies. Repetitive and basic tasks are increasingly being replaced by more creative, collaborative, and logically decision-making career profiles. These changes require employees to quickly adapt to new technologies and also demand that leaders find a new balance between efficiency and human-centered capabilities. Meanwhile, the increasing involvement of AI in decision-making processes is becoming problematic. For instance, algorithmic recruitment and performance evaluations can unconsciously exacerbate workplace discrimination, while the privatization of core technologies can further widen social inequalities. These issues not only affect individual career paths but also challenge societal fairness and stability.

While AI offers tremendous opportunities, it simultaneously exacerbates social inequalities and divisions. Low-skilled workers face higher unemployment risks due to the automation of traditional tasks, while high-skilled workers who master AI gain more opportunities and higher incomes. This trend not only widens income disparities but can also lead to social alienation and conflicts. Moreover, the development of AI is widening the digital divide; individuals and companies that master AI gain more opportunities, while groups that cannot adapt to this change are further marginalized. This gap exists not only among individuals but also among companies, regions, and nations.

In the future, the development of AI will manifest in three trends: First, deeper integration with technologies such as blockchain and digital twins will produce smarter management and high-tech systems. Second, the autonomous evolution of AI systems will transition from "supportive" to "autonomous" decision-making, compelling organizations and systems to adapt. Third, with the progressive development of AI governance frameworks, ethical priorities will increasingly align technological development with justice, transparency, and humanistic values.

The development of AI is not merely a technological revolution but a profound transformation in the way humanity perceives and shapes the world. In this transfor-

 | https://doi.org/10.1515/9783112242728-007

mation, we need both the courage to embrace technological innovation and the will to embed humanistic values.

This book aims to bridge the gap between technological avant-garde and practical demands, helping readers navigate the opportunities and challenges of the AI era and coauthor new chapters for everyday life and professional development.

At the same time, this book also aims to shed light on the extensive penetration of AI in both private and professional life and uncover its implicit ethical and social risks. By analyzing these developments and conflicts, we hope to encourage readers to view AI through a more comprehensive and systematic lens and critically question the boundaries of its application. In this way, we can lay the groundwork for a future model of deep integration between technology and human society. As we enjoy the convenience of AI, we must also analyze the dual nature of technological forces from a systemic perspective and seek scientific and inclusive technological governance. This tension is not only a central theme of AI transformation but also a crucial question mark regarding its role in human society.

To address these challenges, we call for societal enlightenment and political guidance, educational reforms, and the preparation of social security systems to mitigate the negative impacts of AI and ensure that technological advancements are accessible to as many people as possible.

Governments, companies, and social organizations must collaborate to develop sound policies and effective regulations that steer the development and application of AI in a reasonable direction. The education system must be aligned with the demands of the AI era to cultivate interdisciplinary professionals with broad knowledge and innovative capabilities.

Let us jointly advance the shaping of the intelligent society of the future!

Index

 | https://doi.org/10.1515/9783112242728-008

www.ingramcontent.com/pod-product-compliance
Lightning Source LLC
LaVergne TN
LVHW081317110826
845149LV00006B/1530

9783112242711